European Issues in Children's
Identity and Citizenship **5**

Emerging Identities among Young Children: European Issues

European Issues in Children's
Identity and Citizenship **5**

Emerging Identities among Young Children: European Issues

*Edited by Panayota Papoulia-Tzelepi,
Søren Hegstrup and Alistair Ross*

Trentham Books
Stoke on Trent, UK and Sterling USA

Trentham Books Limited

Westview House	22883 Quicksilver Drive
734 London Road	Sterling
Oakhill	VA 20166-2012
Stoke on Trent	USA
Staffordshire	
England ST4 5NP	

2005 © Panayota Papoulia-Tzelepi, Søren Hegstrup and Alistair Ross

First published 2005

British Library Cataloguing-in-Publication Data
A catalogue record for this book is available from the British Library

ISBN-13: 978-1-85856-332-9
ISBN-10: 1-85856-332-1

Designed and typeset by Trentham Print Design Ltd., Chester and printed in Great Britain by Cromwell Press Ltd., Wiltshire.

Contents

Series Introduction:
European Issues in Children's
Identity and Citizenship

Emerging Identities among Young Children: European Issues is the fifth volume in the series *European Issues in Children's Identity and Citizenship*, and is parallel to the sixth volume, *Growing Up in Europe Today*. That collection examines the development of identity during adolescence: this present volume focuses on development from birth to the age of about eleven. Together, the two books present a series of analyses, drawn from writers across the continent, about what is different – and what remains the same – about the way in which children and young people construct their identities in the context of a rapidly changing social, political, economic and cultural Europe.

The series has arisen from the work of the ERASMUS Thematic Network Project Children's Identity and Citizenship in Europe (CiCe). This network has brought together over 90 university departments, in 29 European states, all of whom share an interest in the education of professionals who will work with children and young people in the area of social, political and economic education. The network links many of those who are educating the future teachers, youth workers, social pedagogues and social psychologists in Europe. The CiCe Network began eight years ago and has been supported by the European Commission's Department of Education and Culture since 1998. It is now completing its second phase of development, and planning for a third phase of activities up to 2009.

These volumes have come from our conviction that the changes in contemporary European society are such that we need to examine how the processes of socialisation are adapting to the new contexts. Political, economic and social changes are underway that suggest that we are developing multifaceted and layered identities, that reflect the contingencies of European integration. Children are growing up in this rapidly changing society, and their social behaviour will reflect the dimensions of this new and developing social unit. Identities will probably be rather different: national identities will continue alongside new identifications, with sub-national regions and supra-national unions. Our sense of citizenship will also develop in rather different ways than in the past: multiple and nested loyalties will develop, which will be more complex than the simple affiliations of the past. These two books focus on the emergence of identity, and in the present volume, on how this takes place with our youngest citizens. Though they not have much of an awareness of the concept of 'Europe', the society in which they have been engaged from birth has been moulded by the idea of Europe, and continues to change. The context for the development of identity, the process of socialisation, and the growth of citizenship is different for young children today than it was in the equivalent period of their parents' lives.

Those who will work with children and young people have a particular role to play in this. They will have to help young people develop their own relationships with the new institutions that develop, at the same time being mindful of the traditional relationships known and understood by parents and grandparents, and their role in inter-generational acculturation.

This series is designed to discuss and debate the issues concerned with the professional and academic education of teachers, early childhood workers, social pedagogues and similar professions. They will need to understand the complex issues surrounding the socialisation and social understanding of the young, and to be aware of the similarities and differences in professional practices across Europe. They will need to work with young people learning to be citizens – citizens both of the traditional political entities, and of the developing new polities of Europe.

This volume, the fifth in the series, focuses particularly on the development of younger children's identity. It is thematically linked to the following volume on youth identity.

CiCe welcomes enquiries from potential members of the Network. These should be addressed to the CiCe Central Co-ordination Unit at the Institute for Policy Studies in Education, London Metropolitan University, 166 – 220 Holloway Road, London N7 8DB, United Kingdom.

Alistair Ross
Series Editor

On behalf of the editorial committee: Tilman Alert, Marta Fulop, Yveline Fumat, Akos Gocsal, Soren Hegstrup, Riita Korhonen, Emilio Lastrucci, Elisabet Nasman, Panayota Papoulia-Tzelepi and Ann-Marie Van den dries

Chapter Synopsis

Chapter 1: Introduction: Developing young identities in contemporary Europe

This brief introduction sets out the significance of the early years of life in the establishment of individual identity. Though the identity is of the individual, its construction takes place in a social context, and inevitably this significantly affects the nature of the identity. The structure of the book is set out: the opening section (chapters two to five) consider the emergence of identity in a social context; the second section (chapters six to eight) examine a range of cultural settings and influences; and the final section (chapters nine to eleven) take up important aspects of teaching and learning: books, pictures and the nature of the teaching workforce.

Chapter 2: Different identities and primary school children

The emergence of identity is a social process: interactions with other people have an impact on the beliefs one creates about oneself. Collective identity is a statement about the membership of a certain group who have (or are believed to have) some mutual characteristics. A person may belong to many groups simultaneously thus having many collective identities. These identities can either complement each other, be independent, or oppose each other. The current enlargement of Europe raises the question of a European identity as a sort of supranational identity. The role of school is important in this context for children's understanding of national and European identity: teaching and learning identity and citizenship are concerned with values. Can children in primary school be taught such abstract values as equality, tolerance, solidarity, cooperation and respect? If one is a member of a particular ethnic group and a specific nation, one will tend to have certain representations, thoughts and emotions about them, which will usually be shared with other members of the group. Participating in a supra-national structure may cause a new stereotype of a European identity to develop. The creation of the European Community has led to much current interest in the development of European identity, and to the possibility that this will emerge as a collective identity. Associated with this is the belief that the promotion of attitudes of tolerance and acceptance between members of different nation states will be of significance in preventing conflicts which are rooted in cultural differences.

This chapter reports on a study by CiCe members from eight European countries, focusing on the questions: how children perceive themselves, how do they perceive others, and what do they currently understand about their own nation and Europe? The eight countries involved were Belgium, Finland, Greece, Hungary, Poland, Portugal, Slovenia and the United Kingdom. Few primary aged children understood what the European Union represented. Most of them have heard of the euro and most were also in favour of its introduction. Their knowledge of the parliamentary systems and democratic processes was usually limited to knowledge about voting, though some older children understood the difference between a prime minister and a monarch or president. Most saw themselves as active citizens in the future: they wanted a future society in which there would be technological advancement, greater social justice and a cleaner environment. Understanding European identity is complex, as the identity of each country is underpinned by its own national, political, economic and social diversity.

Chapter 3: Children and Social Identity

This chapter presents the way Denmark welcomes newcomers such as refugees and immigrants. It describes the official policy as can be read it on the Ministry of Refugee, Immigrants and Integration Affairs website, and it presents the way schools and kindergartens in many places try to live up the goals formulated in the *Welcome to Newcomers*. Unfortunately the integration process leaves much to be desired, as is documented in the chapter. Although politicians believe that Denmark is doing everything to integrate newcomers, it shows that newcomers with little or no education coming from countries like Afghanistan, Iran, Iraq, Palestine, Turkey and Somalia face struggles in being accepted, and only high educated newcomers have an understanding of Danish citizenship.

A turning point in the chapter is the question: *will any attempt to define social identity as a formative ideal for children be worth the trouble – or will it just be yet another anachronistic exercise?* This may sound pessimistic, and there does seems to be a political will to make positive changes. New legislation has been introduced, and the whole educational system, from kindergarten to university, has welcomed the challenge and is working on new curricula so that newcomers can learn about the Danish culture, society, politics and citizenship.

Chapter 4: Becoming a cultural personality through the early years

This chapter makes three fundamental points: identity is a process that has both phylogenetic and ontogenetic roots; the different periods in a child's individual development have characteristic activities which influence and construct their emergent identity; and these two points are of significant interest in the pedagogy of small children.

A culture is a system of human values that change – over time and from group to group. Identity – the consciousness of the acting self – is a part of this process of cultural change. The concept of identity can be analysed through different branches of knowledge such as philosophy, the social sciences or neurology. Educational science also contributes to any consideration of the formation of identity in early childhood. The focus of this chapter is on the developmental and educational aspects of the formation of identity in the early years of life.

Chapter 5: Rhymes and citizenship: intercultural tools for the kindergarten

Most European schools today include pupils from various cultures and even the kindergarten school of a small monolingual village will receive echoes of other languages and other cultures through the media and other social and economic links with national and global societies. The presence of this multicultural environment raises questions about culture and cultures, about the relationship between the individual and these cultures, and about the way an individual builds his or her identity in different contexts.

In the kindergarten a careful choice of cultural tools can contribute to building interculturality among a group of children, and allow them to build their own identity and to understand universality. The selection of rhymes can allow teachers to avoid archaisms and stereotypes, including introducing their own culture, and to use them as tools to support diversity, showing children from different cultures that they share the same values. Rhymes allow children to acknowledge individual cultures through activities designed for all children, without identifying anyone as a 'stranger'; instead they can contribute to the development of a common interculture and harmonious citizenship.

Rhymes, songs and playground games are often perceived as a core part of a country's linguistic inheritance. This chapter reflects on two points: first, how can we bring together the enormous possibilities given by these rhymes and by the apprenticeship of shared citizenship? Secondly, how can we extract the core meanings for the development of citizenship from these rhymes and riddles? Cultural features never are isolated or unconnected but are the components of wide systems of behaviour: children's oral culture is connected with rituals, rules, human relations and common life. This chapter considers the impact of simple classroom tools upon apprenticeship, self-esteem and citizenship. Rhymes, songs and riddles can be these tools.

Chapter 6: Young children's identities and first experiences of democracy

Two aspects of early years educational provision that have an inter-dependent relationship to each other are considered here. First, the transition of the young child from the family to the school or a caring institution, which must be carried out with immense care and sensitivity for the child's developing identity. Secondly, and linked to this, is a consideration of how early years settings need to be concerned with aspects of education for democracy, particularly with the young child's feelings of belonging and partnership, and how they learn to understand and follow rules. This chapter asks the question 'which types of education and learning process favour the development of 'democratic personalities' in institutions during the early years?' Although this is an early stage for citizenship education, are there already experiences at this age which prepare young children for citizenship in a democratic society?

Discussion of civic behaviour and living together implies citizenship education. Children's identities, their relationships to others, and their participation in groups are at stake. In a democratic society, children's socialisation involves supporting their individualisation, their autonomy and their social participation. Democratic societies aim to develop individual creativity and critical thinking. This chapter focuses on the socialisation processes in early years settings that are necessary in a democratic society – and *for* a democratic society – and asserts that certain features are necessary at each stage of children's secondary socialisation.

Chapter 7: Children's intercultural identity development through the teaching of languages

This chapter looks at the links between the notion of intercultural identity and competence in children and the teaching and learning of foreign languages. In particular, the authors provide definitions of intercultural identity and seek to establish ways of enhancing it by making children aware of other cultures through foreign language pedagogy. In doing so, they discuss the different functions of foreign languages, as communicative tools and as ways of expressing cultural identity to people who do not share the language. The chapter goes on to present different ways of achieving intercultural competence, by establishing school links between different countries and by creating email projects, and discusses implications for teacher training programmes.

Chapter 8: The development of early childhood education in Iceland: From women's alliance to national curriculum

This chapter gives a glimpse of the history of early childhood programmes in Iceland and places this in context. Icelandic pre-school institutions reflect the threefold purpose of pre-schools in the English-speaking world. Women flocking to the labour market during the 1970s had a dramatic effect on the pre-school system, which was related to the second wave of the women's movement. The need for more pre-schools for all children was on most party political agendas: 'the child in focus' became a common slogan. An overview of Icelandic pre-school legislation is given about the curriculum and the role of the pre-school in the educational system.

All children have right to attend pre-school, irrespective of their parents' situation, whether or not they are single parents or working parents. Today 93 per cent of all three to six year-old children attend pre-school, and 89 per cent of children between one and six years of age. Pre-schools are run by municipalities, and parents pay a fee on a sliding scale. In 1999 a new national curriculum for pre-school was published, which was established from the viewpoint of the rights of the child. A detailed overview of this curriculum is given.

Chapter 9: Children's perspectives on citizenship education in primary education textbooks

Textbooks have been the object of theoretical and empirical research around the world. There has been a particular emphasis on texts for older students, but this chapter argues that primary education textbooks are an important source for the study of ideological and political matters, as well as social learning. They have also recently become a critical source for studying the implementation of reforms

xiv

in schools. This chapter focuses on education in Portugal, and starts with a brief discussion on the role of texts in primary schools today, and how the focus on theoretical and empirical research studies is examining citizenship education studies.

A synopsis of one set of studies and its conclusion is presented, based on an analysis of children's views of their social studies textbooks. This starting point for the chapter is followed by a description of a subsequent replication study that shows pupils' selection of items they particularly like or dislike, and issues that they consider either important or unimportant. The justifications offered for these choices are significant. These give some insight into the challenges which minority group students experience in their integration into Portuguese schools, and point to possible ways of facilitating this. Students' answers are also analysed for their citizenship content, and a separate content analysis has been made of this. Some other subject texts are also examined in mathematics, natural sciences and Portuguese, looking for elements that might contribute to identity formation, global awareness and understanding of cultural, ethnic and other differences.

Chapter 10: Art and Citizenship: a joint venture or a fatal attraction?

What kinds of modern and contemporary art can help support critical citizenship? Can art in a political context include pedagogical and educational meaning, that might contribute to the initiation of citizenship in children? What kind of art is disrespectful of political power? Which art creates negative feelings towards politicians and citizens?

This chapter explores the world of exhibitions and newspapers to try to answer these questions. In contemporary European society art has been transformed from an occasional visual experience into a permanent lifestyle: artists have become agents of social engineering. Art in itself is educational, both in and outside the school. This education is both technical, as in drawing, painting and acting, and moral, as it relates to feeling, evaluating and perceiving. Current curricular obsessions have erased the arts from standard provision in schools, ironically at the very point where it is clear that purely technical and scientific goals do not fulfil the needs of the individual or of society.

Today different kinds of viewing skills are developing as we see different kinds of images. The final part of the chapter analyses deeper aspects of visualisation. The use of philosophy for children establishes a dialogue and interaction between styles of art and processes of mental modelling, and how this contibutes to the development of a visual literacy for citizenship.

Chapter 11: A diverse learning community: the role of continuing professional development

This chapter argues that appropriate provision for young children from a wide variety of social backgrounds requires an approach to staff development that both draws on the cultural capital that staff bring and is responsive to the experiences of the children and their families in the community.

The chapter describes the work in an early years centre, using a case study of a London group of practitioners in a variety of professional roles. It looks at how initial training, experience in practice, and opportunities for continuing professional development should all contribute to the creation of a learning community in which staff can extend their practice and deepen their professional insight. In particular it considers the way in which practitioners from a wide range of backgrounds can develop a broad and responsive curriculum that supports children and families from diverse cultural, linguistic and ethnic groups in an inner city area. The link between the London practitioners and Danish social pedagogues is described, and the significance of this contribution to the learning community is discussed.

1

Developing young identities in contemporary Europe

Alistair Ross, Panayota Papoulia-Tzelepi
and Søren Hegstrup

The Jesuits had a saying for it: 'Give me the child till he is seven, and I will give you the man'. This became the *leit motif* for a series of UK television documentaries that started in May 1964, called *Seven Up*. The director of this first film, Paul Almond, selected a fairly random group of seven year-old British children, and interviewed them about their backgrounds, their lives, hopes and aspirations. One of the assistants on the film, starting to learn the trade of film-making, was the 22 year-old Michael Apted, who went on to make *That'll be the Day, Coal Miner's Daughter, Enigma,* and *The World is Not Enough.* Apted directed a follow-up film of the same children at fourteen (*Seven plus Seven,* 1970) and then made a third film after a further seven years, *21* (1977) ... and then *28 Up* (1985), *35 Up* (1991), *42 Up* (1998). Michael Apted is about to start filming *49 Up* and has promised to keep following and filming the participants, if they are willing, as long as he lives.

Together, the films follow the lives of fourteen individuals as they grow up, become adult, and move into middle age. They are ten boys and four girls; six are working-class, four middle-class, and four from wealthy backgrounds; thirteen are white, one is black. Have their ambitions and attitudes been set in motion, if not carved in stone, in the early years of life? In some respects, the Jesuit maxim is substantiated: there is a certain inevitability as some of the children grow into roles that seem to have been predestined at the age of seven. In other instances the axiom is challenged: some refocus and reorientate their life.

One boy, Tony, from the East End of London, says at the age of seven that he wants to be a jockey. At fourteen he's working as a stable boy, and at 21 he's riding at Kempton Park alongside Lester Piggott. But at fourteen he is also thinking laterally: if a full-term career with horses is not possible, he will become a London taxi driver. At 21 he says, 'All I understand is dogs, prices, girls, 'the Knowledge'[1], roads, streets, squares and Mum and Dad and love. That's all I understand – all I want to understand.' At 28 he is a taxi driver, and he still is at 42. But by this stage his parents have both died, his marriage has nearly failed and he has moved from the inner city to the suburbs: 'I've done as well I can go – I think this is about the limitations for me now.'

The case of Neil apparently contradicts this sense of predestination. Intellectual and thoughtful at seven, he wants to be a bus driver, so that he can tell passengers what to look for out of the windows. At seven and at fourteen he lives in a middle-class Liverpool suburb: but by 21 he is a squatter in London, and at 28 he is homeless in the wilds of West Scotland. By 35 he is physically downtrodden and destitute, living in a council house on the Shetland Isles. At this point, Bruce, another participant in the series, gets in touch with him and offers him temporary accommodation in London. By *42 Up,* Neil is a Liberal Democrat councillor for a London borough, has taken an Open University degree and plans to teach English as a foreign language: he says he is 'looking to the future' for the first time in his life.

Bruce is at a private school at seven; by 21 he is studying mathematics at Oxford. He gives up a career in insurance in order to teach in London's East End. At fourteen he was explaining that he does 'not agree with the Conservatives' racial policy', and by 42 he is head of Mathematics at a multi-racial, multicultural secondary school.

2

'The child is father of the man,' Wordsworth wrote in *The Rainbow* (1888). *Seven Up* and its successors suggest that perhaps it is not so straightforward: the parentally determined social class of the child is more likely to determine its destiny. The three young upper-class public school boys are sure of their social track. John announces at seven that he 'reads *The Observer* and *The Times*'[2], and that he will proceed through elite schools to University and into the professions. Charles refused to appear in any of the films after he was 21, and is now a senior television executive; and Andrew has a senior legal position. 'Just because you had the opportunities it doesn't mean you're necessarily going to pull through,' he argues at 42 – though all these upper-class children *do* 'pull through'.

The working-class children pull through in a different way. Three of the girls are from a London east-end school. Lynne marries at nineteen. 'You do think, Christ, what have I done?' she says at 21, and is still with her husband at 42. Jackie also marries at nineteen and Sue at 24: they have now both been through a series of relationships and all three are still struggling to bring up children, with or without help from older relatives. These three seem, of all fourteen subjects, to have the strongest relationships with their own children. Sue says that she wants her kids to have 'really satisfying careers', something she's never had. But the working-class children's aspirations are limited. While John at seven effortlessly predicts his passage through higher education, Paul, living in a care home, asks 'What does university mean?'

Chances are not wholly determined by the age of seven, as some of these cases demonstrate. Where they are predestined, is this a consequence of the social class and position of the child's family? Or, as the Jesuits suggest, is it the result of what education can do between birth and seven? The Jesuits were not the first to make such a proposition: the father of humanism, Desiderius Erasmus, had suggested in the early years of the sixteenth century that 'a man is not born a man, but becomes one' (1979, p31). Human beings, he argues, can improve when given a liberal education based on free will, which, he argued, even children possess.

Identities are not simple or determined in contemporary societies. The seven year-olds' sense of themselves is not fixed, and new aspects of identity will supplement, complement, and may even replace previous descriptions. In modern society we express different and contingent identities as we move between various social settings. This book focuses on the development of identity by young children up to the age of eleven in Europe, but does not presume that the identities achieved within this temporal and spatial framework will remain fixed. The current personalities and expressions of these young people, who will be the leaders of their societies in the Europe of the 2050s, are only in part being determined by the social educators of the present. We do not know what else will shape their identities by the time that they reach mid-life, but there will be changes, differences and developments in many aspects of their characteristics and personalities by that time.

Nevertheless, what social educators provide for young children is critical for their future. Lacan, working from a psychiatric basis, identified the importance of what he called the 'mirror stage' in the development of a child's sense of identity, which occurs during the first two years of life (1982). He suggested that the child's emerging sense of self is always created with reference to the 'other.' This other could be the child's own 'image in the mirror' – the 'mirror stage' – or a sibling or a friend, or one of many alternative models the child might associated herself with (following Freud's explanation of narcissistic identification).

However, Lacan also held that the mirror stage was not simply part of the process of developing a healthy sense of identity but was the source of a fundamental alienation in the individual's idea of self. The notion of self created during this stage was oriented in the 'fictional direction' of an other, who is seen as a powerful potential rival to the self. Therefore, the identity that develops at this point inevitably includes a destabilising and hostile aggressiveness. Human identity is thus developed in an inter-subjective context, within which alienation and aggression are the norm, not the exceptions.

4

Lacan identified *méconnaissance*, or misperception, as the core of the *ego*. We only have knowledge of ourselves as a *self*, as an independent body that is distinct from others, through systems of representation, predominantly language. But because of the nature of representation and of subjectivity, this self-recognition contains losses and absences. Language comes before and is a determinant of subjectivity: it is not function of our identities and desires; rather our identities and desires are functions of language.

The contributions to this book examine the development of early identity from the more empirical basis of professional practice in educational settings. Cross-cultural studies of children's upbringing, such as Richards and Light (1986), might suggest that there is a much stronger link between identity and culture than Lacan proposed. Jerome Bruner makes the link explicit: 'education must help those growing up in a culture to find an identity within that culture' (1996, p38).

Learning, including the learning of identity, involves the social construction of meaning (Edwards and Potter, 1992) and discursive psychology, based on social interactionism and traditional developmental psychology, explains human behaviour as a series of communicative social acts and actions: as a conversation. This approach gives a conceptual frame for understanding development through interactions and dialogue (Harré, 1998; Harré and Gillett, 1994). Harré argued that we need a better understanding of how an individual constructs his or her personal identities through social interaction (1998). Stables (2003) points to the pioneering work of Andrew Pollard (1985) in examining classroom interaction:

> the groups of pupils he came to refer to as 'Jokers' ... were often the most successful in school, for the very reason that they took a more proactive role than other students in *negotiating* the progress of lessons; in effect, they took greater roles in the discourse of the classroom. There is surely scope for research into the conditions under which students are encouraged into, or discouraged from, becoming Jokers, or moving into other kinds of roles within the broader group dynamics of the class. (Stables, 2003, p12)

Pollard and Filer have subsequently developed a substantial Identity and Learning Programme, on which they report in part in *The Social World of Children's Learning* (1996) and in part in *The Social World of Pupil Career* (1999). They outline the various forms of strategic action available to primary-aged children as they develop their identities as learners around the key concept of conformity. A variety of contextual factors, both in and outside the school, are shown to impact on the children's identities in the classroom, particularly relationships between children and teachers.

Edwards and Mercer show how cognitive socialisation and individual identity can be achieved through the effective use of language in teaching (Edwards and Mercer, 1987). Building on Vygotsky, they demonstrate why 'schoolwork' needs to be analysed in the context of broader interaction. Comparisons of classroom discourse in Britain with those elsewhere in the world have been explored by Alexander (2000), who shows how national and regional contexts affect classroom dialogue. Informal teacher-pupil talk is more dominant in England and the USA than in France or Russia.

The explicit European dimension of this book is reflected in the range of countries and cultures of the authors of the various chapters we include, who are from the UK, Denmark, Greece, Slovenia, France, Iceland, Finland, Portugal and Belgium.

We have organised this volume into three broad sections. The first section examines the emergence of identity in the early years, raising theoretical questions as well as offering empirical experiences.

In the second chapter Pergar Kuščer and Prosen explore theoretical aspects and categories of identities from a broad research field. They also present the findings of an empirical research on children's understanding of national and European identity and of children's tolerance to the 'different other'.

In the third chapter Hegstrup presents the unsuccessful effort of the integration policy in Denmark. Although refugees and immigrants are offered courses in the Danish language and culture, it is particularly children and young people from other ethnic backgrounds who are having serious difficulties in the integration process.

In the fourth chapter Korhonen and Helenius describe the fundamental points in development of identity. The focus of the chapter is on the developmental and educational aspects of information in the early years of life.

In the fifth chapter Dinvaut reflects on value of children's use of rhythms, songs and playground games in the kindergarten. She points out that children's oral culture is connected with rituals, rules, human relations and common life.

The second section of the book approaches issues of culture as they relate to the formation of identity in childhood.

Fumat presents the relationship that a kindergarten education should offer in terms of curriculum and human resources to contribute to the development of the child's democratic values.

Spinthourakis and Sifakis, responding to the changing political and cultural scene of Europe, explore the links between intercultural identity and competence in children and the teaching and learning of foreign languages, stressing that languages should not only be approached as communicative tools but also as carriers of culture.

In chapter eight Dýrfjörd presents a view of the history of the early childhood programmes in Iceland. She analyses the new curriculum for pre-schools, designed specifically to protect the rights of children.

The third section is devoted to the important issue of education and identity development.

De Freitas stresses the importance of text books in education, especially in centralised systems in Europe or elsewhere. She also presents children's own views on several Portuguese text books, including those related to the development of national identity and identifies what children like and dislike, and what they think of as useful for learning or not.

Verkest explores the use of cartoons in development of citizenship. He argues for the importance of visual literacy in post-modern society and for the scientific role of cartoons, using an example of a

7

didactic use of a cartoon in the classroom.

Finally, Maggie Ross explores the importance of staff development, suggesting ways in which educators trained to reflect the cultural diversity of the population. Stressing both the need to recruit from the linguistic and ethnic diversity of the community, she also shows how staff can be supported to support the development of diverse identities in young children in early years settings.

Notes

1   'The Knowledge': the technical and geographic knowledge of London streets that taxi-drivers in London must posses and demonstrate in order to gain a license to trade.

2   Two elite UK newspapers, at that time.

I: The Development of Identity

2

Different identities and primary school children

Marjanca Pergar Kuščer and Simona Prosen

The emergence of identity is a social process. Interactions with other people have an impact on the beliefs we create about ourselves. From the beginning of life, a child is a social being, capable of interactions with others (see Korhonen and Helenius, this volume). A newborn baby may be considered to be autistic but a change happens between the ages of six and ten weeks. At this moment a child turns outwards and enters a symbiotic relationship with a significant other, a person who is important, usually the mother. Through this process the child becomes at one with the mother, who mirrors the behaviour and emotions of the child, thus giving him or her a feeling of security that will last throughout his/her lifespan (Praper, 1999). The skills achieved through these social interactions eventually become internalised and the child thus becomes increasingly self-sufficient and independent.

In his theory of psychosocial development Erikson (1968, in Zupančič, 2004) defined identity as an organisation of all the past and present identifications, characteristics, wishes and tendencies that are believed to represent a person. Chen *et al.* (2004) make a distinction between three different aspects of identity by the individual, the relational and the collective self. The first of these, *individual identity*, represents a person as 'an entity separate or independent from others' (p91), the second, *relational identity*, describes a person in relation to significant others, and the third, *collective identity*, describes how a person is a member of a group or a collective.

Collective identity is a statement about the membership of a certain group who have, or are believed to have, some mutual characteristics (Ashmore *et al.*, 2004). It consists of a set of

* cognitive beliefs regarding that group such as stereotypic traits and ideological positions,

* affective aspects, evaluating and assigning an emotional significance, and

* behavioural components, such as language usage.

The characteristics assessed can be either ascribed – such as ethnicity or gender – or achieved – such as occupation or political party (Deaux, 1996, in Ashmore *et al.*, 2004).

A person belongs to many groups simultaneously, thus having many collective identities. These identities can either complement each other, be independent, or oppose each other (Kovačev, 1996).

With the current enlargement of Europe, the question of a European identity as a form of supranational identity has arisen. The role of school is important in this context: teaching and learning identity and citizenship are concerned with values. Can children in primary school be taught such abstract values as equality, tolerance, solidarity, cooperation and respect? In such areas students will be affected not only by the method of teaching but also by the teacher's personality. Personality is reflected in all dimensions of human behaviour and activity, including values. A teacher's understanding that every child must feel that they are accepted in the class should be only on the declarative level, but should reflect a real situation (Fumat, this volume). There is no doubt about the importance of experiences and learning opportunities in primary school. If a child feels respected, he or she sees the importance of learning and of developing good relations with his or her peers (Pergar, 2001). Lessons should simultaneously promote children's sense of belonging, their understanding of one another, and their academic achievement. For schools to play a role in the development of identity, both national and European, they need to have some understanding of how children perceive themselves, how they perceive others and what they currently understand about their own nation and about Europe.

Development and culture

Throughout their development each child learns to live in the culture in which she or he is growing up. The term 'culture' is used here to include everything that human society produces and shares, from languages, myths and beliefs to family patterns and political systems. Human behaviour is the product of interaction between the individual's biological heritage and the learning experiences of the specific culture in which he or she happens to live (Robertson, 1989).

How a child sees and understands this reality depends on his or her environment, on interactions with other people, and on her or his age. The child plays an active role when they internalise experiences from the environment. She/he not only incorporates the behaviour of their parents, siblings, peers and teachers towards them, but also, from the very beginning, tries to get be accepted as a member of a group, first in a very immediate sense, and then by using learned social strategies. If this acceptance does not happen, conflict may arise, the nature of which will depend on the developmental stage. Children vary in their degree of sociability, as a part of their inherited temperament, which is a source of individual difference (McIlveen and Gross, 2002). The resolution of each developmental conflict will depend on the interaction of the individual's characteristics and the support they receive from the social environment. Each person regulates their behaviour in interacting with others according to her/his subjective perception and feelings. But a child builds his/her understanding of the world not only on direct experience, but also on the experiences of others which are passed on to him or her through language. According to Vygotsky's (1986) theory of the social formation of mind, language is the most effective means for internalisation of social interactions. He believed that social relations become converted into mental functions, not that development proceeds toward socialisation (Driscoll, 1993).

11

During the pre-school years and through play with their peers, children acquire the skills, ideas and values that are crucial for growing up. When first entering school children are curious and learn quickly to be competent in mastering new skills and to think logically if the topic is sufficiently concrete (Piaget, 1977). At school children develop the capacity to work and cooperate with others but, according to Erikson's psychosocial theory (1950, in Berk, 1994), a sense of inferiority will develop if negative experiences lead to feelings of incompetence. The teacher's role in this is very complex: it is far broader than merely delivering the curriculum. Teachers are individuals, with various personality traits, and these are expressed through their teaching and their attitudes towards their pupils, and will also be reflected in relationships between pupils. Enthusiastic, creative and communicative teachers know how to include less popular pupils (Pečjak, 1989, Pergar-Kuščer, 2002). From the child's perspective, his or her peers' reactions to his or her physical, intellectual and social abilities are of great importance. Experiences gained through their time in school are crucial for self-evaluation and identity formation. From the very beginning it is important for the teacher to give each child chances to excel in front of her or his school peers. The teacher's behaviour and reactions to pupils' interactions can lead towards either a tolerant and creative atmosphere or to competitiveness and stress atmosphere in the classroom.

Identity development

Two processes are linked to the origins of a child's identity formation. The first is self-perception, which appears soon after birth and includes the knowledge that the body is constant, that experiences with one's own body are different to those connected to others, and that these experiences can be influenced by action (Kobal, 2000). The second process is self-consciousness, appearing between fifteen and eighteen months of age, when speech and self-conscious emotions such as guilt, shame and pride occur (Smrtnik, 2004).

Horvat and Magajna (1987) defined four phases in identity development in the pre-school period: the use of a personal name at around two years, increased autonomy which is shown through actions and

12

feelings of pride, a more complex idea of the self, *ie* 'that's me and that's mine' at approximately four years of age, and the verbalisation of sensations about oneself at five or six.

During the years spent in school a distinctive academic identity emerges. It appears first in the structural model of self-concept, as presented by Shavelson and Bolus (1982, in Kobal, 2000). Their assumption was that self-concept was differentiated and based on a hierarchical structure throughout social development. General self-concept is divided into academic and non-academic, the latter consisting of social, emotional and physical self-concept. In the academic sphere, further divisions were made for specific subjects, as a child does not necessarily perform equally well in mathematics and history.

Adolescence features many developmental tasks which a growing child must undertake to become an adult. These tasks, as specified in Horvat and Magajna (1987), include searching for an identity, accepting bodily changes, developing sexuality, adjusting relationships with colleagues and parents, making educational and vocational decisions, and forming personal, moral and ethical values. One particular developmental task, identity formation, might be perceived the most important of all.

A critical author in the field of identity research in adolescence is James Marcia, whose ideas derive from Erikson's psycho-social theory. He argues the existence of four identity statuses (Marcia *et al.*, 1993): identity diffusion, foreclosure, moratorium or suspension, and identity achievement. These statuses differ around two criteria: the presence or absence of the exploration of alternatives, and commitment. In this context, people who achieve identity have explored many alternatives and committed to the chosen one. Foreclosed individuals have committed without exploration, while those in a state of suspension are still exploring, and have not yet committed. Identity diffusion is described as a lack of commitment and of exploration. The major characteristics of these statuses, as described in Kobal (2000), are that identity achievement means having a clear self-concept, high self-evaluation and moral judgement level,

13

mature social relationships, a high level of autonomy, and an interest in complex tasks. Foreclosure means low anxiety, a self-concept that changes because of environmental influences, autocratic values, a low level of autonomy, cognitive rigidity, and a dissatisfaction with institutional education. Suspension includes a high level of anxiety, a clear self-concept, quite high levels of self-respect, a level of autonomy, an interest in complex tasks, and dissatisfaction with institutional education. Diffused identity also implies a high level of anxiety, a self-concept that changes because of environmental influences, unstable social relationships, and a low level of autonomy.

Collective identity

Markus and Kitayama (1991, in Kobal, 2000) describe two models of what they call self-system: interdependent and independent. The first, interdependent system is used to sketch a self-system developed within a culture, in which conformity, belonging to the group and co-operation are highly appreciated. The interest of a group is more important than the interest of the individual. The independent system, however, would prosper in a culture that stresses individualism, competition, self-centredness and independence.

Another distinction made between different aspects of identity is described by Chen *et al.* (2004): the individual, relational and collective self, which were described earlier. Some further distinctions should now be made between ethnic, racial and national identities, all of which are included in the 'collective' category.

Identity development in general is influenced by the process of separation/individualisation and by the degree of connectedness to the family or others who are close. This can also be observed in the development of collective identity. Apart from these inner factors, ecological perspectives have also to be considered, such as the transmission of values and beliefs within a society (Hale, 1991, in Lloyd, 2002).

Throughout development the child, adolescent and adult selves will combine into a cohesive self. Ethnic identity is one of these identities, referring to the emotional, behavioural and cognitive connectedness to a particular group, and its formation goes through defined developmental phases (Phinney, 1990, in Kim-ju, and Liem, 2003):

Unexamined ethnic identity: little attention is focused on ethnicity, so that preference for the prevailing culture is indicated,

Search for ethnic identity: in exploring issues of the culture of origin rejection of the prevailing culture may develop,

Achievement of ethnic identity: individual ethnicity is perceived as valuable, and is used to resolve conflicts with the dominant culture.

Is the emergence of a particular collective identity due to the perception of 'being similar' to other members of that collectivity, or is it the perception that the group as a whole is different from other groups (Musek, 1994)? A related question concerns the development of a collective/ethnic identity: what happens when two or more different cultures meet, exposing unfamiliar contents of other people's ethnic identities and to the perceptions held by others of our own ethnicity? This later may sometimes be even harder to deal with. Is what happens here more similar to the 'melting pot' metaphor or to the 'amalgam'? Introducing the term *acculturation* to the discussion may help to answer these questions.

Redfield, Linton, and Herskovits (1936, in Rudmin, 2003) defined acculturation as

those phenomena that occur when groups of individuals with different cultures come into continuous contact with subsequent changes in the original culture patterns in either or both groups (p3).

Rudmin (2003) presented a fourfold theory describing the possible relationships between two groups, usually referred to as the majority and the minority groups. These are:

* a positive attitude towards both the majority and the minority group

* a positive attitude towards the minority, but a negative attitude towards the majority group

- a positive attitude towards the majority, but a negative attitude towards the minority group

- a negative attitude towards both groups.

Berry (1990, in Kim-ju, and Liem, 2003) called these positions: *integration* or biculturalism, meaning identification with both cultures, *separation* or exclusive identification with the culture of origin, *assimilation* or exclusive identification with a new culture and *marginality* or deculturation, meaning the absence of identification.

The *stage theory* of acculturation with respect to ethnicity was introduced by Cross *et al.* (1991, in Ashmore *et al.*, 2004), and proposed five ideological positions or stages in the formation of a new collective identity:

- pre-encounter: when the ethnic group is not considered an important element of self-concept

- encounter: when certain events bring ethnicity into focus and when it can no longer be overlooked

- immersion-emersion: when views are exaggerated as a feature of being in an intermediate state

- internalisation: feeling more comfortable as a member of a certain group

- internalisation-commitment: when ethnic identity becomes a consistent guide to action, yet is not overemphasised.

National identity
Belonging to a particular ethnic group and a specific nation means that one will tend to have certain representations, thoughts and emotions that will usually be shared with other members of the group. Musek (1994) identified this as 'group consciousness' or 'group ideology' (p15). He suggested that only when national identity is achieved would a nation be ready to be included in interstate structures, such as the European Community. Joining such a supranational structure creates a new stereotype of a European identity

16

(Chryssochoou, 2000). Such a stereotype is shaped by a people's perception of their own national group and its position within Europe. The boundaries of sub-groups do not need to be eliminated for there to be a reduction of perceived bias between groups: it is sufficient that the super-ordinate group begins to acknowledge the existence of a two-group society. However, the question of how and whether a supra-national identity of a European will emerge remains unanswered.

National identity is connected to:

- *National consciousness*, which is based on national loyalty and a sense of belonging to a state that ideally coincides with a nation. In multi-ethnic and multi-national states the overemphasis of typical national characteristics may cause intolerance towards members of minority groups.

- *National character* includes the representation of perceived typical and long lasting characteristics of members of a particular nation. Prevailing personality traits and life-style are a part of this. When comparing members of a nation, differences between individuals are greater than differences between the members of sub-groups (Musek, 1994).

- *National stereotypes* are simple cognitive schema, which store information in an easily accessible form but can lead to biased social information processing, giving misleading information about the homogeneity of the group.

A theoretical background to the formation of collective identity

Several theories try to explain the process of collective identity formation, using the term 'social identity'. Tajfel and Turner's 1979 (Ashmore *et al.*, 2004) *Social Identity Theory* assumes that

> experiencing oneself as a member of a group provides participants with an instant and meaningful collective identity that is experienced as emotionally significant. That is, mere categorisation is enough to trigger in-group-favouring behaviour , in-group loyalty and adherence to group norms (p84).

17

An alternative theory of collective identity formation is the *Self-Categorisation Theory* (Turner *et al.*, 1987, in Hogg and Williams, 2000), in which

> development of social identity theory ... refocuses attention on the categorisation process. Social categorisation transforms the basis of social perception, so that people are perceived not in terms of their unique individual properties but in terms of shared in-group or shared out-group category attributes. Perception is 'depersonalised' in terms of in-group or out-group prototypes that are formed according to the principle of meta-contrast (e.g. maximisation of the ratio of perceived intergroup differences to intragroup differences (p88).

Stryker (1980, 1987, 2000, in Hogg and Williams, 2000) introduces an *Identity Theory* that originates in the sociological tradition. He argues that society specifies certain positions and roles which people use for their social self-definition.

The outcomes of collective identity formation

Several phenomena are connected to the formation of collective identity:

- *Physical and psychological well-being.* The common belief that there is a connection between negative stigmatisation of a particular social group and the lower self-esteem of its members is not always supported (see, for example, Crocker and Major, 1989, in Ashmore *et al.*, 2004). Another hypothesis holds that the collective identity can have a buffering function which promotes personal well-being (Sellers *et al.*, 2003, in Ashmore *et al.*, 2004).

- *Academic achievement.* Steele (1997, in Ashmore *et al.*, 2004) introduced the theory of the *stereotype threat*, which focuses on the possible prediction of performance by ethnic identity. Ways of measuring the effect of collective identity on school performance are questions about attendance, consultation search, choice of curriculum, and the availability of resources such as books and computers. These are possible indicators of power relationships between groups, political and economic factors and cultural values and norms, which are contextual variables of collective identity research.

- *Interpersonal relations.* Possible outcomes connected to collective identity are prejudice and discrimination and anti-social behaviour, directed towards the out-group and pro-social behaviour to the in-group members. The phenomena of nationalism, racism and xenophobia can be the negative consequence of extreme and allegedly positive attitudes toward a particular group, such as the nation. Eidelson and Eidelson (2003) present individual and group representations of five core beliefs which can become dangerous if they become too strong: superiority, vulnerability, injustice, helplessness and distrust. Each of these might lead to extremely negative outcomes. There is evidence that increased contact with out-group members can lead to a decrease in biased perceptions held about them (Thompson, 1980, in Baumeister, and Leary, 1995).

- *Organisational commitment* and *civic and social engagement* are the final collective identity related outcomes. The first of these is connected to different identifications at work, to do with organisation, unit and work role, and the second is expressed through different kinds of social action such as donating, volunteering and demonstrating.

Multi-dimensional conceptualisation of collective identity

Ashmore *et al.* (2004) present several distinctive constructs of a collective identity that occur on an individual level:

Self-categorisation depends upon the combination of a stimuli, a situation and a perceiver (Tajfel, 1979, in Ashmore *et al.*, 2004) and means the 'identifying self as a member of, or categorising self in terms of, a particular social grouping' (p83). There are three levels to the categorisation: placing self into the social category, perceived goodness of fit with the category and perceived certainty of self-identification.

Evaluation is defined through the attitudes one has toward the social category in question. It has public and private aspects: the former concerning the attitudes of the individual towards the group to which he/she belongs and the latter about the judgements the person thinks that people have about the group.

Importance: membership of a particular group may either be very important or of no importance at all to the individual. Explicit importance is indicated by a subjective report of how valuable membership is seen to be of the group in a whole self-system, whereas implicit importance is placement of a particular collective identity in a hierarchical structure of all collective identities. Placement may not necessarily be conscious, but if it is high the content of the collective identity is continually within reach of an individual in normative situations (Chatman *et al.*, 2003, in Ashmore *et al.*, 2004).

Attachment and a sense of interdependence occur when a mutual fate is perceived but only when a person is treated as a group member (Gurin and Townsend, 1986, in Ashmore *et al.*, 2004). In this construct a distinction has to be made between an attachment to the group as a whole and an attachment between members. When an individual is a member of a particular group, the interconnection of self and others can blur the boundaries between the two through introjection (Rosenberg, 1979, in Ashmore *et al.*, 2004).

Social embeddedness is a more objective and external construct than the previous category. It can be made effective more easily when the specific collective identity is implicated in a person's everyday social relationships.

Behavioural involvement describes the direct actions that are taken which imply a certain collective identity category, such as when ethnic identity is largely maintained through the use of language.

Content and meaning are shown through several phenomena: self-attributed characteristics which are the overlap between the group and perceived personal characteristics; ideology, which is beliefs which concern group experience in both a historical and current society context; and narrative, which is an internalised story about

20

oneself being or becoming a member of a certain group and about the group itself. All the concepts presented within the collective identity are combined in various ways, opening up a broad field for creative research work.

European collective identity: perspectives of the European children

The creation of the European Community has led to much current interest in the development of European identity and to the possibility that this will emerge as a collective identity. Associated with this is the belief that the promotion of attitudes of tolerance and acceptance between members of different nation states will be of significance in preventing conflicts which are rooted in cultural differences.

A comparative study by CiCe members from eight European countries focused on the following questions: how do children perceive themselves, how do they perceive others, and what do they currently understand about their own nation and Europe? (Krzywosz-Rynkewiccz *et al.*, 2001, 2002). The eight countries were Belgium, Finland, Greece, Hungary, Poland, Portugal, Slovenia and the United Kingdom. The aim was to examine the social processes within the national context at the same time as comparing social phenomena connected with identity across countries. Around two hundred children between eight and eleven years of age were interviewed and each was given a number of focused tasks. From photographs of children from many different ethnic groups they were asked to identify those most like themselves, and to talk about the life styles they thought the other children might have. They were asked to say which of these children they would prefer to sit near them in class, which they would choose to spend the weekend with and what they might learn from them. With regard to European understanding, they were asked whether they considered themselves European and were given a list of countries, including all of those in this project and three others: Japan, USA and India, and asked which of these countries were in Europe and what they knew about them. Further questions concerned how they would describe themselves to a child from the USA and to whom their families would donate money. In an attempt to have an insight into their knowledge of their own state's democratic processes, they were asked about their country's rulers and political processes. A final question focused on children's values and the kind of future they would like. The interviews were recorded and analysed using constant comparative technique. (A detailed description of the methodology employed can be found in Krzywosz-Rynkewiccz *et al.*, 2001, 2002, presented at the CiCe conferences in Brugge (2001) and Budapest (2002).

The aims of this study were to determine and describe four key areas:

• Children's understanding and perception of their national identity

• Children's perception of tolerance and differences

• Children's understanding and perception of European identity

• Children's understanding of European citizenship.

Children's understanding and perception of national identity
Most children had a strong sense of their own national identity, associated first with their language, then with food, customs, games and clothes. For some children, from mostly the monocultural countries, skin colour seemed to be a determinant of nationality. Many of the older children indicated an awareness of a common history, heritage and special monuments. Some children from ethnic minority groups did not identify with the host nation or were not sure of their nationality. But there were also answers such as: '*I'm three-quarters Jamaican and one quarter British.*' (girl, aged eleven), or '*My children would be British for a start but then if I teach them Greek they will be a little bit Greek.*' (girl, aged seven). Children whose parents spoke a different language at home were less sure of their identity.

Children's perceptions of tolerance and difference
The main difference noted about children from other cultures or countries was their language, followed by outward appearance,

22

customs, food and clothes. Some children saw those from other countries as being better off than themselves. Some saw others as being poorer materially, because they did not own computers or televisions and lived in areas where wars took place. Many children hold stereotypical or factually incorrect views of children from other parts of the world, in particular of Africa. Many had not travelled outside their own country and seemed to base their knowledge of children from other countries on information from tourists, from what they had seen on television or what they had learnt in school. In many cases their knowledge of people from other countries was based on negative or narrow stereotypes. In spite of little first-hand knowledge, nearly all were very receptive to meeting and working alongside children from other countries. However, in some countries a few children indicated the beginnings of xenophobic attitudes. Some answers, such as '*I think those children could have bad habits and get into trouble more. I think there's enough people in this school anyway*' (boy, aged eleven, in a rural all-white school) were rare. A very small minority in each country would not welcome children from other countries. The majority would welcome children from other cultures or countries into their school to learn their language and culture. Most would like to spend the weekend with a child from another culture, but some were concerned about what their parents' views might be.

Children's understanding of European identity

The children who saw themselves as European most often mentioned the euro or their country's location in Europe as evidence for this. Some identified a European heritage, referring to a common past. Some children were ambivalent about creating closer links with Europe. Their knowledge of the characteristics of individual countries in Europe was very poor and often based on stereotypes.

Children's understanding of European citizenship

Few children understood what the European Union represented. Most of them have heard of the euro, and most were in favour of its introduction. Their knowledge of the parliamentary systems and democratic processes was usually limited to voting. Some older children understood the difference between a prime minister and a monarch or president. Most of them said that they did not learn about these things at school, though they would be willing to do so. Most saw themselves as being active citizens in the future. They wanted a future society in which there would be technological advancement, greater social justice and a cleaner environment.

Understanding this kind of identity is complex, as the identity of each country is underpinned by its national, political, economic and social diversity. The study described some common and other more specific perceptions and understandings by children of nationality, tolerance, difference and citizenship, to identify the existence of a European identity. The results do not identify the national origin of each specific answer, although some interesting national differences appeared. The question is whether these differences originate in the differences between nations, since the countries represented in this study differ in their respective multi or mono-cultural and democratic traditions. However, differences identified might be no more than a reflection of specific differences in age, schooling system, or family backgrounds, that are of equal importance in every nation. Further exploration in this area is suggested to avoid the mistake, common in cross-cultural psychology research, of overemphasising differences between groups and neglecting inter-individual variability. Studies with more representative samples of children from different nations would be useful, and the research conducted in Greece (Spinthourakis, 2004) and in Slovenia (Tratnik, 2003) are a step in this direction.

Setting these results alongside some of the different constructs of collective identity described above, it is possible to conclude that some children categorise themselves as Europeans, but that this is mostly a characteristic of the older children and is a consequence of the extent of their geographical knowledge. The children's evaluation of European identity, and of its importance to them, is not clear: this may be because the abstract nature of such an identity is greater than the children's capacity for concrete cognitive functioning at this age. Attachment and a sense of interdependence occurred in the answers of some of the older children, who mentioned common historical origins and heritage but generally in relation to their own nation of origin. They emphasised the importance of behavioural involvement in their construct of a collective identity but did this around their own nation: children perceived their sense of national belonging as occurring mostly through their use of a common language and sharing of common customs.

These findings stress the importance of fostering greater communication between children in Europe, whether by email, school visits or specific European Union funded projects such as the COMENIUS programme. These activities may promote attachment, interdependence and behavioural involvement to the emerging concept of a European identity. Cogan and Derricott (2000, in Krzywosz-Rynkiewicz *et al.*, 2002) indicate that we need to educate young people who can work co-operatively, accept cultural differences, think critically, defend human rights, solve conflicts non-violently and participate in politics.

Many different kinds of identities have been discussed in this chapter but there are others, perhaps even more abstract and distant in nature, such as democratic world identities and human identities (Musek, 1994). Nevertheless, the research discussed in this chapter is an important counterpoint to the occurrence of sometimes exaggerated expressions of national or ethnic identities.

3

Children and social identity

Søren Hegstrup

It is tempting to introduce a chapter about children and social identity by asking if any attempt to define social identity as a formative ideal for children will be worth the trouble, or will it be yet another anachronistic exercise?

> Social identity is a collective concept, which attempts to describe the formal civil, political and social rights and duties of any citizen in society. But the concept also comprises the way in which rights and obligations are practised in everyday life, social identity is inclined towards society and social issues rather than the idea of citizenship which solely includes the legal dimension of our rights and obligations. Mads Meier Jæger (*Velfaerd i Europa*, 2000)

Following and applying Mads Meier Jæger's definition of social identity, the objectives of the *Folkeskole*, the Danish municipal primary and lower secondary school (*Folkeskole* Act (Denmark, 2003, Objects, item 3) gives a clear answer to the question of whether it is conceivable that social identity can be a formative ideal:

> Item 3. The Folkeskole should endeavour to acquaint pupils with Danish culture and to contribute to their understanding of other cultures and of human interaction with nature. School should prepare pupils for participation, co-responsibility, rights and obligations in a society with freedom and democracy. The school's teaching and entire daily life should therefore build upon intellectual liberty, equality and democracy.

This is the only legal text in Denmark that provides the opportunity for educational practitioners to tackle issues such as upbringing, teaching and training for the purpose of social identity and citizenship.

Can we learn from history?

There is much misery in the world in which children grow up, and much discord which justifiably causes anxiety for parents and teachers alike. Many children's and youth establishments experience massive difficulties in keeping up with change. The *avant-garde* seems to be out of sight, and many practitioners feel part of an '*après-garde*'. There is probably nothing new in this. Children are not what they used to be, but they never were what they used to be anyway. The view of children over the last thirty years has been characterised by an atmosphere of hopelessness, probably originating in the sociological hopelessness that culminated in the 1970s. Somewhat provocatively, one might subsequently say that the therapeutic supermarket of the 1980s sought to make good the damage caused by this hopelessness. As we now know, this did not succeed, but then the new world order of the 1990s created enthusiasm and optimism.

That was the decade when became acceptable once again to look back a little further than just the previous generation, or the last twenty-five to thirty years. It again became interesting to discuss whether the grand narratives had actually died. And the subsequent debate confirmed that those who read the grand narratives could own up and refer to their significance. Philosophical dimensions of the theory of teaching were once more nourished and they blossomed. Lars-Henrik Schmidt's MA about the history of ideas mentions the poetry of pedagogy in *Dansk Pædagogisk Tidsskrift* (1999) and discusses the rebirth of the theory of social education in *Tidsskrift for Socialpædagogik* (1998). Peter Kemp has now become professor of educational philosophy, taking the route to education from philosophy by way of theology. His pedagogical excursion could be seen as the same as a journey from Aristotle to Comenius – or from Rousseau to Kant – and today from the hopelessness of the 1970s to the optimism of the turn of the millennium: there are endless opportunities for analogy. It was clear that, once again, it had become the most critical task of pedagogy to put the identity formation debate on the agenda, as well as to mark its ethical dimension. Kant's *Über Pädagogik* (*On Education,* 1899) was first translated into Danish only in 2000. Løgstrup's *Etiske fordring* was dusted off and opened afresh (second edition, 1991) and the *enfant terrible* of modern philosophy, Feyerabend, struck again with *Anything goes* (1975). Giddens formed modern sociology (1993) followed by Beck's theory of the risk society: *Don't be afraid of the dangerous traffic – you are the dangerous traffic* (Pedersen, 2003). The turn of the millennium had become a wonderful pivotal point. We could look back and evaluate whether the Swedish popular philosopher, Ellen Key, was right when she pronounced in 1902 that the twentieth century would be the child's century – or was it Henrik Jensen when he called it the *Victim's century* (*Offerets Århundrede,* 1998) towards the end of the same century? Two or three world wars have not made it easy to be a family with children. The twentieth century did not become the child's century: on the contrary, children became the victims, as they always do, victimised in wartime as in peace. This has been documented by both psychology and sociology, with thousands of statistics to verify the stark figures. Henrik Jensen's point is that modern man has been brought up, taught and trained to be a victim, whimpering and reproachful, never satisfied, making a virtue of the perceived injury committed against him and his helplessness.

Yet out of this wretchedness, as if by magic, optimism and faith appear some time after 1989. There is discernible progress. Dion Sommer (2003) manages to dismiss psychology: only post-1992 psychology is any good. It is again acceptable to read sociology at university. Huge numbers of new texts in psychology and sociology are written. It took ten years to wind up and close *Danmarks Lærerhøjskole* (The Royal Danish School of Educational Studies), which shook up middle-range educational training courses in teaching, nursery teaching, social work and health. Everyone has to come to terms with all things new, the new paradigm and the new order. We meet again on the third way, from Durkheim and Husserl to Giddens. The political and economic world studies Giddens, and it was fashionable to work on ethical accounts. And then, suddenly, the impossible happens: two aeroplanes crash into two high-rise buildings. It was not the flutter of the butterfly's wings but, as in chaos theory, the effect is the same. Historic events which cause war and discord always worsen the conditions in which children and adolescents grow up. They create desperately bad and difficult conditions for children and adolescents to develop any sense of social identity. Occasionally war and discord might strengthen national identity, but history shows unequivocally that a mobilisation towards discord is far more likely. The following sections look at initiatives which have been designed to safeguard the next generation of world citizens, to develop their rights as citizens and to create a socially cohesive population in the post-war world.

The Treaty of Rome

The Treaty of Rome of 1952 was to be the basis of the new agenda in Europe. The huge number of declarations and conventions on which the European Union member countries agree are all intended to safeguard access for all to the good life. The rights of children are especially to be safeguarded: any kind of exploitation or suppression of children is prohibited. All children have rights; ethical codes are designed for professional work with children; children must receive education and have equal rights to further training. This is not an un-documented thesis: it is common knowledge, routinely used by politicians, especially at election time, whether local, county, national or European.

There are numerous development programmes in the European Union designed to achieve these goals. Some programmes are directed at education. Everyone working in further and higher education knows of COMENIUS, SOCRATES ERASMUS, and, more recently GRUNDTVIG. All these programmes are named after people in history who have contributed significantly to education, training and the formation of minds. The official goal is to work towards a common European dimension and to agree on good practice. All educational institutions participating must submit their 'European dimension' and a 'policy statement' that sets out what they consider to be 'good practice'. When these have been agreed the institution can enter into contractual relationships with other institutions within the 25 European Union member countries and the remaining candidate countries. Possibilities also exist for development programmes with countries outside Europe. It is still apparently undecided what exactly constitutes Europe: some believe that Turkey does not belong to Europe, even though Israel is free to participate in the European Song Contest. Some suggest that Russia should be invited to be closer to Europe, whilst others suggest that the post-communist countries' eastern borders should be a new Iron Curtain.

The Bologna agreement

The Bologna agreement was the first attempt to harmonise higher education within the European Union. The European Credit Transfer System (ECTS) point system sought to harmonise the level and length of educational training. Academic degrees, including their titles, will be harmonised: in future, and with few exceptions, we shall have just three academic degrees, the BA, the MA and PhD. This will cause certain problems, which remain outside the terms of reference of this chapter. The DPU (The Danish University of Education) and the SDU (University of Southern Denmark) plan to establish an MA in Citizenship and Social Identity. One area to be treated is Children and Social Identity. The concepts of citizenship and social identity are very well-defined, both etymologically and historically, when dealing with citizens who are *adults and of age*. In Denmark, this means people over the age of eighteen. However, the social identity and citizenship of *children* is much less clear. A number of national and international children's and youth organisations exist, who are working for children's rights and legal status, but the social identity of children does not seem to be on the agenda.

Over the years many people have had strong views on the upbringing of children and adolescents and the formation of their social identity. Intentionally, if not in practice, they were addressing the ultimate goal, which is similar to the relationship between the ethics of obligation and the ethics of utilitarianism. We might adopt a Kantian view and believe that children are innately good and capable of distinguishing good from evil. The categorical imperative can also be applied for children. But the road to adulthood, to life as a citizen with a discernible social identity, is a process of training and exercise, as the child becomes aware of and understands discipline, culture, moral standards and civilisation. Acquiring moral standards and civic values leads to the cultivation of social identity and citizenship (cultivate from the Latin *cultus* – enabling something to grow).

Citizenship in Denmark

Denmark was the first country in the world to introduce a personal ID number. Everyone is automatically allocated a Central Person Register number at birth (CPR). This also applies to anyone who moves to Denmark to take up residence, other than as a tourist. If you are a Danish citizen, you automatically have the right to vote in elections. Two groups are not allowed to vote: children and those without Danish citizenship, such as refugees and asylum seekers. The road to citizenship for each of these three categories is patience and good behaviour: this is the Danish way. If you are Danish by birth, institutions will guide you a long way, helped by family and the media. Asylum seekers and refugees do not have such an easy time, but the Ministry for Integration has included a sort of welcome on its website explaining exactly what constitutes being Danish. With a little goodwill, it could be read as an integration manual.

Welcoming the newcomers (WWW.inm.dk)
(Denmark, Ministry for Integration, 2004)

Dear new fellow citizen.

Starting a new life in a new country is likely to bring great changes. You will meet new people and new systems. You will encounter norms, values and traditions which may be different to those you are used to. The initial period, therefore, may well be filled with challenges and feel quite overwhelming.

In Denmark, we believe that the diversity and multiplicity which you and others bring to our country will result in innovation and dynamism, and we hope, therefore, that you will wish to engage yourself actively in the society of which you are now an integral part...

The land of cyclists

Denmark is one of the countries in the world with many cyclists. During the rush hour in the cities you will observe rows of cyclists – many carrying children – on their way to and from work and institutions.

In most places, the traffic is designed to accommodate cyclists. There are cycle roads and signposting reminding motorists to consider cyclists crossing the road...

Children and adolescents

The majority of children below the age of six are in daycare institutions, for example, a childminder's, nursery or kindergarten or spending time with other children in some way during the day. There are several options. The local authorities are responsible for providing daycare, but the type and number will differ from one local authority to the next. The most common ones are:

- Childminder. The child is looked after in a private home, with other children, by a childminder who is approved by the local authority. Especially for children from birth to three years of age

- Day nursery, an option for children between birth and three years of age

- Nursery school, an option for children of three to six years of age

- Outlying nursery school, which means that the children spend their day in the country or in the woods

- Integrated institution. For children between birth and six years, all cared for together

- Free choice: An option where the local authority provides a grant to parents who choose to have their children looked after privately

...

Holidays, special days and festivals

During the year there are a number of holidays and special days that are marked by giving the children a day off school. Most adults will be off work and the shops will be shut for all or part of the day. On holidays there will be a church service in the *Folkekirke* (the national church).

The most important holidays are celebrated in connection with the three great festivals, which are Christmas celebrating the birth of Christ, Easter which is centred around the crucifixion, death and resurrection of Christ and Whitsun which celebrates the Holy Spirit.

There are numerous traditions connected with these festivals, especially at Christmas. For most people the festivals are good occasions to be with family and friends.

Other holidays are:

• New Year's Day, 1 January

• Prayer Day: originating from a number of prayer days now celebrated on the fourth Friday after Easter

• Ascension Day where Christians celebrate Christ's ascension

The most important special days are:

• 1 May, the workers' international day of action

• 5 June, Constitution Day where we celebrate the Kingdom of Denmark's constitution: we got our first written constitution in 1849

Children's birthdays

Many parents of children of nursery and school age invite their child's friends or classmates to a birthday party. Some invite only the girls or only the boys. Layer cake, buns and hot cocoa or lemonade are part of a traditional Danish children's birthday party, as is singing the birthday song and playing games. The children invited are expected to bring a present for the birthday child. If you are in doubt about the kind of present to buy and how much it should cost, you can ask other parents.

Irony and humour

In Denmark, humour is a significant way in which people relate to one another. Many also make use of irony. This means that the tone at a work place sometimes may seem rather harsh. People may say things to each other which sound coarse and which you, as a newcomer, may find somewhat alarming. But often it is just an indication that you are friends and respect each other, even though you also tease each other a bit.

(translated by the author)

A commentary on the letter of welcome

The integration manual quoted above is probably reflects the best of intentions of the minister and the civil servants. It is interesting in two ways. Can Danes actually identify with the 'typical' Danish characteristics that are described? Is it possible for the newcomer to be able, by the process of socialisation, to adopt the same characteristics? If so, which agents of socialisation will best secure this internalisation: social workers, nursery teachers, teachers, nurses or the police? Or might it be volunteers like scout leaders, sports instructors or sports leaders? Finn Thorbjørn Hansen offers some conclusions in his contribution to *Uddannelse* (2002), where he focuses on the contrast between being accommodating to the youngsters' interest in being true to themselves, and the question of whether a Socratic conversation (Saran and Neisser, 2004) can prevent groups and cultures from ossifying into holding rigid opinions and displaying group egoism. Indications suggest that all attempts to prevent or minimise the formation of ghettos among immigrants in major cities in Denmark have failed.

A curriculum for pre-school institutions

The educational work carried out in pre-school institutions has never been put on the curriculum in Denmark. Stig Broström from the Institute for Curriculum Development at the DPU has his roots in nursery education. He argued for developing and implementing a curriculum in pre-school education. This has finally happened and from August 2004 all daycare institutions and childminders must define curricula objectives (Denmark, 2004, www.socialministeriet. dk). This replaces the former vague formulations, which were intentions merely to provide children with a 'good time', the closest previous definition of a curriculum for pre-school institutions.

The following clauses describe the objectives and principles for work with pre-school children (see box on page 36).

From mid 2004 there has been an additional requirement that all nurseries should detail their objectives for educational work with pre-school children. Childminders must also formulate educational

4.1 General objectives and main principles for public sector education for children and parents

To provide all children and adolescents with the best conditions in which to grow up and develop, while paying due attention to the needs of young families and allowing for a combination of working life, family life and childhood.

The family is the foundation for bringing up children, and children are the responsibility of their parents.

The public sector has overall responsibility for creating a positive framework and is obliged to protect children and adolescents against abuse and lack of care, and to support parents in their parenting role.

All who have a need have equal rights to services.

4.2 Daycare provision: Objectives for daycare provision

Daycare provision contains three parallel objectives, of a social, educational and caring nature. Daycare provision should promote children's development, well-being and self-reliance by:

- Cooperation between the parents and the daycare institute
- Care and support in acquiring social and general skills
- Strengthening each individual child's development and self-worth
- Contributing to a good and secure childhood
- Stimulating the child's imagination and language development
- Providing the opportunity for play and learning, free expression and socialising
- Giving the child a voice and teaching responsibility
- Facilitating an understanding of culture (Danish and others)
- Knowledge and experience of nature and the natural environment
- Displaying a preventive and integrating attitude
- Contributing to providing special support to children with special needs.

objectives: the Act requires the local authority to be responsible for establishing educational objectives for the daycare sector as a whole.

The task of formulating corporate objectives had previously caused teachers endless worry. Søren Smidt, of RUC (University of Roskilde), documented in his PhD thesis (Smidt, 1999) the difficulties in formulating corporate objectives, and how these objectives do not reflect the reality experienced by children in daycare centres.

The lines of battle have been drawn in this debate on educational objectives: Stig Broström (DPU) thinks that the requirement to set objectives is a divine gift to teachers, and that this finally makes it possible to describe in precise terms what children in a pre-school institution should learn. Others think it nothing short of a calamity that educational objectives for children must now committed to paper. Jan Kampmann, Professor of Childhood Research at RUC, is a confirmed opponent: he thinks that such educational objectives are of no value, arguing that children will automatically learn what they need. The journal of Børne-og UngdomsPædagogernes Landsforbund (IBUPL), *Børn og Unge* (Jensen, 2002), has followed the debate between Broström and Kampmann since the Act on educational objectives was passed in the *Folketing*. This debate has allowed teachers to see the issue from both sides.

The Act stipulates that the objectives must set minimum goals for areas of work for daycare institutions as follows:

- **Language**: knowledge of vocabulary, pronunciation, the written language, rhymes and jingles, the existence of figures and letters and their use, and basic IT and communication

- **Social skills**: learning to establish relations with others, to feel and express empathy and respect for others, to function in social contexts, and to be aware of democratic values

- **Personal skills**: exploring concepts such as self-worth, setting limits, imagination, creativity, feelings, decision making, motivation and perseverance

- **Nature and natural phenomena**: learning respect for and knowledge of nature and natural phenomena, understanding concepts such as weight, form and number

- **Aesthetic expression:** sensory awareness of music, art and drama, of using materials such as clay, awareness of creative and cultural expression and achievement

In the context of competencies relating to social identity, it is interesting to examine the *social skills*. Will the daycare institutions, with their cultural ballast of several hundred years, manage to meet the requirements of the Act, which significantly contradicts their traditional approach?

Henriette Kjær, the Minister for Social Affairs, published a set of *Comments on the Bill* (Kjaer, 2003), in which she justified the inclusion of educational objectives in the Act on grounds that it was necessary to break the circle of social custom and inertia. She quoted foreign research which suggested that establishing educational objectives will lessen the danger of social imbalance but provided no sources or references for this work in her *Comment.* Nevertheless, there is a healthy debate among researchers, educationists, teachers and others interested in educational work with pre-school children, with several major conferences arranged on the subject. What do daycare institutions need to prepare pre-school children for? What is the overall task of the *Folkeskole*?

The object clause in the *Folkeskole* Act (Denmark, 2003, www.uvm. dk) stipulates that children should be brought up 'in the spirit of democracy and intellectual liberty'. No mention is made of imparting skills of citizenship or developing social identity. But Mads Meier Jæger's definition of social identity makes it clear that the intention of Article 1 § 3 is for the *Folkeskole* to internalise social identity as a formative ideal. The Folkeskole's goal is:

38

Chapter 1

The *Folkeskole's* objectives

§1. The *Folkeskole's* task is, in cooperation with parents, to further pupils' acquisition of knowledge, skills, working methods and ways of expression ultimately contributing to the comprehensive personal development of each individual pupil.

§2. The *Folkeskole* should seek to provide a framework for experience, activity and involvement such that pupils will develop cognitive skills, imagination and the inclination to learn giving them confidence in relation to their own possibilities and basis for decision making and action.

§3. The *Folkeskole* should endeavour to acquaint pupils with Danish culture and to contribute to their understanding of other cultures and of human interaction with nature. School should prepare pupils for participation, co-responsibility, rights and obligations in a society with freedom and democracy. The School's teaching and entire daily life should therefore build upon intellectual liberty, equality and democracy.

A Commentary on the Objectives

Examining the *Folkeskole* objectives clause highlights that daycare institutions now have the task of preparing children for school life. For many people working in or around the world of education, the central element or goal is the final sentence in §3: 'the School's teaching and entire daily life should therefore build upon intellectual liberty, equality and democracy'. To achieve this the school must be able to prepare pupils for participation, co-responsibility, rights and obligations in a society with freedom and democracy.

The Social Services Act (Denmark, 2004), which governs daycare institutions, stipulates that they should encourage children's development, well-being and self-reliance through:

• The child's participation and co-responsibility
• Developing the child's understanding of culture (Danish, as well as others).

This articulation leaves no doubt that daycare institutions must teach children participation and how to assume responsibility, which is repeated in what is taught at school later on. Children are first expected to learn about Danish culture in order to understand other cultures. This is precisely what does *not* clearly emerge in the daily work of some daycare institutions. In 2003 the Integration Secretary, Bertel Haarder, appointed a think tank (Denmark Ministry for Integration, 2004) to suggest provisions for a bill on how daycare institutions and *Folkeskole* should solve this problem. A survey by Hedegaard (2003) documented that both daycare institutions and the *Folkeskole* are selective in their implementation of this policy, maintaining refugees and immigrants within their respective cultures. They integrate neither adults nor children *into* Danish society: quite the reverse. The idea that their social identity should include both their original ethnic background and their Danish identity fails miserably. A third kind of identity is being developed: the identity of the ghetto, now being formed in the refugee centres.

Danish society does not give refugees a 'proper' reception (Hegstrup, 2004). They find it extremely difficult and humiliating to be interviewed by Danish police on arrival in Denmark and they are unhappy with the reception they get at refugee centres. The first positive welcome they meet in Denmark comes from fellow refugees, who have already spent some time at the centres. They recognise the problems and do something about them. Danish language courses and courses in Danish culture and society are offered to adults and children, but to no avail. One explanation for this is that the motivation to learn Danish and acquire some knowledge of Danish culture and society is not manifest until asylum has been granted: there may be a long wait, provoking negative attitudes towards Danish society. After an initial stay in a refugee centre, most refugees, once they have been granted asylum, will be allocated a home in an immigrant ghetto. These contribute little to developing an understanding of Danish culture or of democracy. The negative attitude towards Danes, initially conceived in the refugee centres, will be deepened and will contribute to the emergence of a ghetto identity, incommensurate with a Danish sense of social identity. Many of the families from an Islamic background do not wish their children to attend daycare institutions, and believe that children should be raised by their mothers in their homes. These mothers are offered courses in Danish language and culture at the day high schools, but many of then find this an unpleasant experience, incompatible with their culture. Mothers therefore often hurry to pick up their children from the daycare institution, as soon as their own language tuition finishes. Another survey has shown that a number of ghetto children do not learn Danish because only the mother tongue is spoken at home. Older sisters and brothers, who should be able to speak Danish, do not teach their younger siblings, partly because they may not be able to, and partly because it may be considered of low status to speak Danish. Bertel Haarder's think tank therefore recommended obligatory Danish tuition in the daycare institutions for children from two and a half to three years of age, and tests in classes 2 and 7, and introducing tests to identify those who need additional special tuition in Danish. Critics have responded by pointing out that this will add yet more tasks to the work of daycare institutions and school, and contribute to further marginalisation and exclusion.

While there are good intentions to address these issues, the situation in some ghettoes appears to be polarised between two cultures, with no dialogue taking place between them (Yüksekkva, 2004). This is a bad situation for any child to grow up in, for both Danish or minority ethnic children. In some cases when a crisis occurs daycare institutions and schools appear utterly incapable of action, but similar institutions, in similar instances, are miraculously capable of success.

Three Questions

Whichever institutions address the issues and attempt to resolve them, three questions remain:

What is a pre-school child?
Who are the experts?
What can we use their expertise for?

To answer these questions: there are explanations offered not only by contemporary psychological thought, as outlined earlier, but also by theories from the fields of sociology, ethnology, anthropology, philosophy and theology.

Childhood is constructed

Per Schulz-Jørgensen (2002) argues that childhood is a construction, which becomes evident through:

- the separation of childhood from adulthood

- the professionalising of the task of bringing up children

- the declaration of friendliness towards children

He refers to the American psychologist, Roger Hart, who wrote

> 'Children are without doubt the most photographed people in our society – but also those least listened to'. The modern view of children is often contained in expressions like children are freed, free to be different – and free to make their own choices. This they do, then. But they do more than that: they choose for themselves – and choose themselves. The personal project. The individualized lifestyle. The ready-made identity (Schulz-Jørgensen, 2002).

Children are self-centred, self-reliant, competent, superficial, spoilt: they are zappers and members of the 'me-generation'. They are different because they are engaged in a project about *themselves*. There is great distance between the *Folkeskole*'s objectives and this kind of reality. To accept Schulz-Jørgensen's conception of childhood as a construct leaves little room in a child's perception of society for the development of social identity. The more likely scenario is a generation of children who, in establishing their active identity, develop a kind of anti-social identity, which the adult world is expected to understand and unconditionally accept. The professional task of bringing up children is therefore often felt to be an uphill struggle. The professional child-rearer has to guide the child in becoming a good citizen, as well as allowing the child be responsible for her or his own learning, this later being an example of rather anti-social behaviour that may have serious consequences for intellectual liberty, equality and democracy.

Who are the experts?

The Danish psychologist, Dion Sommer, has both written and talked of pre-1992 developmental psychology being useless and of mere historical interest (2003). Many nursery teachers feel inspired by Sommer and at several institutions providing training for pre-school teaching he has attained guru status. Sommer is preoccupied with Daniel Stern's developmental psychology theory and its modern view of children, in which children are 'capable' of much more than was believed possible by established developmental psychology (1998). Children are capable of entering into emotional and social relations at an early age, so it is important to formulate learning objectives to assist daycare centres to create opportunities for children to form relationships both with other children and with their teachers. A new educational method has been developed, which is known as 'relation teaching' (Refshauge and Bak, 2001): relationships have become the new mantra in daycare institutions.

What can we use their expertise for?

A study of the corporate objectives of daycare centres shows that almost all have set out plans to provide children with opportunities to develop *relation competency* (Smidt, 1999).

One reason for this is that children and their parents now spend very little time together and so relationships outside the home become more important in the child's social life. But the greater social life – in society at large, of which the child is also part – is not addressed in this new educational movement. In summary, it could be said that the social-psychological and social-educational dimensions are missing from the debate on the definition of social identity as a goal for daycare institutions (Hegstrup in Gustavsson, 2003).

Conclusion

Teachers will have hard times ahead. Democracy does not seem to be valued by the next generation. Educational institutions themselves suffer from a deficit or, at worst, – a total lack of democracy (Hegstrup, 2003). Children of as young as pre-school age would rather be stars for a day than relate on terms of equality to their peers. Many children live their institutional lives as if they were a preview to 'the' great night in the television studio. This can be very evident when visiting a pre-school institution, where the children's choreography comes directly form the world of the stars and they provide the set themselves. Chain stores such as *Fætter BR* and *Toys r Us* have caught this development and many of the toys purchased for nurseries are perfect accessories for the television studio set. The essence of democracy is that the majority should encompass the views of the minority but 'knee-high' democracy is experiencing hard times. The middle-class ideals of loyalty, the social democratic ideal and solidarity are unknown quantities. Løgstrup's (1905-1981) old doctrine: 'life is basically unjust – therefore solidarity is a necessity' is not getting through to children and adolescents. Either injustice does not exist or children and adolescents have adopted inequality as part of their parameter of values. When it becomes possible to zap socially and emotionally, as described by Roger Hart (in Schulz-Jørgensen, 2002), then the institution is hardly a uniform environment in which children and adolescents will assimilate the set of values necessary for modern social identity and citizenship. At worst, an antagonistic conflict will arise between what the teacher perceives to be the values for good citizenship and children who drop them fast: an old and well-known oedipal conflict.

The Danish priest, teacher and social castigator, N.F.S. Grundtvig (1783-1872) (Reich, 2002) compared the four phases of human life to the four seasons. It is food for thought that he placed childhood in the winter quarter which, in Denmark, is cold and dark.

4

Becoming a cultural personality through the early years

Riitta Korhonen and Aili Helenius

This chapter makes three fundamental points. First, identity is a process that has both phylogenetic and ontogenetic roots. Second, the different periods in a child's individual development have characteristic activities, which influence and construct their emergent identity. Finally, these two points are significant for the pedagogy of small children.

A culture is a system of human values which change, over time and from group to group. Identity, the consciousness of the acting self, is a part of this process of cultural change. The concept of identity can be analysed through different branches of knowledge, such as philosophy, the social sciences or neurology. Educational science also contributes to any consideration of the formation of identity in early childhood. This chapter focuses on the developmental and educational aspects of the formation of identity in the early years of life.

Layers of the self: identity as a cultural concept

The renowned neurologist, Antonio Damasio, studied the layers of the self (2000, p156-185), uncovering the neuroarchitecture of consciousness. He identified three different constructions, each of which he argued was needed to serve consciousness. The oldest of these, called by Damasio the *proto-self*, exists because bodily processes are represented in the nervous system, which constantly controls them. Although these processes are unconscious, disturbance of the control structure affects the complete loss of consciousness. Such a total loss does not result from the disturbance of other centres affiliated with the consciousness.

The second level of Damasio´s model of consciousness is closely related to object manipulation. Damasio calls this level a *core self* and *core consciousness*. Its simplest characterisation is being simultaneously aware of an object and of oneself handling this object. Giving this attention to the object further clarifies the picture of the object in the mind. Damasio suggests the brain constructs a picture – a non-verbal secondary representation – of the changes which occur when the object is experienced. The parts of this picture then combine the acting self and the secondary maps of the object.

When we speak about human identity we need yet another level, termed *widened consciousness* by Damasio (2000). This widened consciousness is possible because of the cortex; it is built up of autobiographical memories, constructed and reconstructed with the help of language. The identity of a human person thus has its prerequisites in this autobiographical memory, which contains important pieces of our identity for us, building memories such as our own name, our family details, where we were born and things we like. These autobiographical memories are used in the brain as though they were objects or things. Every time these objects are processed through the memory, so also is the self; these memories are pulses of the core identity.

Damasio's studies were made with adults, and he has not followed the process of the development of consciousness with children. The sociologist Norbert Elias (2000, p290) has pointed to this as problematic, in that by only studying the final results in the adult, the methodology hides the process of becoming. We are encouraged to consider the individual and society as separate entities, even though they need each other and could not exist without each other. Elias suggests that this concept should be researched and theorised in the study of the process of becoming.

We tend to think that identity develops as a part of the brain's activity, from the inside out, as the child's neurosystem ripens. But identity does not grow in this way: its roots are cultural. With development, identity undergoes structural changes through important transitional periods. This chapter specifically focuses on three periods in the early years of life, before school age:

- the *new born* period, when the activity of the child is still conducted jointly with the mother or caregiver

- the *second half of the first year*, at the point that the child shows a profound interest in manipulating objects

- the period of *imaginative play*, which begins at the start of the second year and lasts through to the school years.

Culture as a cradle of learning

The founder of cultural historical theory, Lev Vygotsky (1998, 1997; see also Veresov, 1999), concluded that the higher psychical processes in humans, as differentiated from the lower primary processes, are internalised social relationships, mediated by signs, which have replaced the lower functions. Human higher psychical activity is thus culturally mediated. The use of objects as tools, and of language as a social tool, are important processes in this mediation. Culturally mediated activities lead to changes in the construction of a personality. It may be that, in the transitional periods from one structure to another, the functioning of the adult is of special importance.

Each nation has its own culture of values, norms and habits, and these traditions influence the development of a child's identity, including behaviour, citizenship and partnership in a European or a global culture. The environment of the child's family transfers culture to the child. Cultural behaviour, such as how to use a spoon, are learned in everyday life (Valsiner, 2000; Addo, 2001) Children learn traditions and social manners through the life of their family and through social occasions.

The wider support of society, such as institutionally organised day care and education in kindergarten, is now able to support and help families in these educational tasks. Children often come to these social institutions from different ethnic backgrounds which makes enculturation richer. Multiculturalism creates demands for the teachers: they must be skilful in organising pedagogical activities and developing each child's relationships to maximise the benefit of the richness of these cultural impacts.

Identity: a project before birth

Turning from theory to practice, and to the three phases in the child's life before school age identified above, we need to focus on the individual child as a member of her or his society. Althusser suggests (2000) that human individuals are already subjects before their birth. He refers to family behaviour and habits during pregnancy, such as deciding on a name and to the rituals immediately following birth. The infant is welcomed as a person, and is dressed like his or her peers, specifically as a boy or as a girl. From conception the identity of the individual develops in the cultural conditions of the family. The voice of the mother already sounds in her or his ears, the music that she listens to can be heard by the unborn child; and she or he participates in the rhythm of the her daily life. When the baby comes into the outer world, the social situation begins a new phase of development.

Early games as experience for identity

All cultures contain a rich supply of traditional songs, games and riddles (see Dinvaut in this volume), which are of interest to both researchers of early interaction and to teachers of young children (Mahler and McDewitt, 1982). They encapsulate many of the rules of human communication which will be introduced to the child through emotional contact and repetition (see Dinvaut in this volume). Joint attention by parent and child to the details in these rhymes and games starts to build a prototype of enculturation (Bruner, 1982).

Playing these games, the parent and the child are in face-to-face contact: they can easily observe each other. The eyes of the parent may be covered and suddenly uncovered, with a few repeated words, often including the name of the child. The child is physically rocked up and down, forward and backwards, and these actions help the child to understand the meanings and rhythms of the repeated words. These early interactions in the positive development of the self of the child, and the child's future identity are of great importance. Traditional games and songs have both cognitive and social meaning: they teach for the child the elements of communication before speech and singing and playing them with an adult promotes close relationships.

The second half of the first year

From being at one with the primary caregiver, as the child gains the ability to move he or she separates physically from the adult. A new period of development begins with this ability to move, as it does for the caregiver. If identity has been attached warmly to a parent, the child will have the courage to move away from the adult and seek her/his own path, and make her/his own discoveries.

Six Finnish mother-child pairs were videotaped each month over a three-year period (Jakkula, 2002; Helenius, 2002). As with children in earlier studies (Eppler, 1995), the children were seen to be interested in handling concrete objects during the second half of their first year. This is before meanings of the objects become part of the child's understanding. Any assumption about the meaning or purpose of these objects was *preceded* by coordination of sight and finger movement. Shortly after beginning to crawl, all the children began to follow their finger tips, exploring objects with their eyes and engaging in palpatory searching. At an earlier stage, the same children had used their hands and fingers for searching, but their eyes did not follow their hands. The coordination of sight and hand movements is important, following Damasio: core consciousness consists of two separate processes: that of the perpetrator, and that of the object concerned.

It is remarkable that this palpatory searching begins shortly after the child has begun to move herself/himself about the rooms of her/his home. There are many reasons for the child to move forward a stage in his/her psychological development and in the development of consciousness at this point: mothers of children of this age report that the child now must be constantly followed everywhere. The adult must intervene in problematic situations as the child tries to reach and manipulate everything around him, such as putting dirty shoes in his mouth. It follows that the child is also becoming aware of his own will as separate from, and different to, that of his mother, his father, and other people. The individuation of the child has its starting point here. It also follows that the child is able to assume cultural meanings for the objects in his surroundings. The adult mediates meaning through their actions and their language. Through imitation, the child assimilates the *use* of the objects, and un-consciously learns their cultural meaning.

This separation of the self also means that the child acquires a primary understanding of the possibilities of difference (Perner, 1991). First comes the two mode understanding ('me – not me', 'here – not here', *etc.*). Many of these opposites existed in the games and songs, such as 'up-down' and 'fast-slow'. Now the child can also observe these attributes and descriptions about the objects s/he is manipulating. This develops to mean even more. Soon the child can separate the present from the past, taking a picture of what was experienced in the past and acting on it now, in the present. Imagination opens up.

In this phase, the dyad (child-and-object, or child-and-mother) grows into the triad: child-object-mother. The period of joint attention begins (Jakkula, 2002) and, through imitation of the use of objects as adults use them, no longer only as manipulative objects to put in the mouth, the child moves on to imitative and imaginative play.

The pattern of play used in relation to objects is that the child first uses an object according to its cultural meaning and then later, through role-play, uses it according to some personal sense, as part of his or her play idea. These experiences are important parts of the child's autobiographical self. Having acquired the ability to use secondary representation, the child is ready to begin imaginative play and this becomes part of her/his way of life, and a mediator of personal identity.

A child in a day care culture

Some children begin their day care at a very early age, before they are three years of age. The development of their identity is influenced by the children and adults around them. These day care activities impact on both the child's and the group's developing identity. Teacher and children together create their own way of life in the kindergarten with rules and manners produced through regularly repeated activities. Each child brings parts of his or her family culture to the life of whole group. This cultural pluralism contributes to the quality of the learning environment offered by the kindergarten.

Teachers are accountable for being aware of and able to perform their roles as educators who are responsible for the social environment that supports the formation of each child's identity. Every child has a right to develop emotional balance, self-confidence and self-respect, and to develop respect for the opinions of others. The group is therefore important for the child: in the group she or he can feel part of a whole. The teacher's obligation is to consider how different levels and types of group activity can be used to enrich each child's development and socialisation (see Maggie Ross in this volume).

What is the optimum learning environment for the individual child? Whilst the curriculum is culturally determined, it is the educators who must decide its main goals and activities. They must have a high level of awareness and of morality in making decisions, so that they can make sure that the programme serves the child's needs. The teachers also develop their own self-awareness in this process: Althusser stressed that personality is formed through culture and cultural activities – 'there is the production of the self as an object in the world, the practices of self construction, recognition and reflection, the relation to the rule, without which no subjectification is produced' (Althusser, 2000, p22-23).

Adopting a role to prove other identities

Imitation is a way to learn to understand oneself, as well as to understand other people, and early childhood is the period of strongest imitation: it is soon combined with imaginative play. The child is able to move into the imaginative realm, where s/he can overcome obstacles through the imagination, even when reality hinders her/his strivings for adult-like activity. Before the age of three, the child is already able to assume a role.

A role can be seen as a plan for the personal activity of the child: it also enables complex planned co-operation with other roles in the same play scenario. Although the play is imaginative, what happens is real: the child's actions and co-operation with others, the emotions and the dialogue. The imitated cultural models and rules are also real. These roles show the child's development of character. Drama play is an opportunity to open new ideas for the child's self-identification (Korhonen, 2004). The kindergarten teacher can widen the child's interests, and by creating a digital portfolio can document these experiences and communicate between home and kindergarten about developmental issues (see Kankaanranta, 2002).

Learning in a group
The curriculum of early childhood education highlights the need for an environment that supports the child's development and learning, balancing teaching activities, work, play and everyday chores (see Korhonen, 2002). The curriculum builds the daily functions of a group of children so that they support the natural developmental needs of the individual child. Within the group, the shared activities of children – their social skills, playing together and the relationship between children and adults – become important competences in their education. Siraj-Blatchford and Clarke (2000, p12) emphasise how the promotion of self-esteem encourages interactions, encourages discussion about how the child and others feel, and draws the child's attention to other people's points of view. This contributes to learning constructive ways to solve conflicts and to promote co-operation, rather than to encourage competition.

In building possibilities for group learning, certain phases can be predicted in the development of relationships between children and in the growth of their attitudes and motivations for learning. The quality of co-operation and of the dialogue between teachers and parents affects the group identity. Respecting each other in the kindergarten greatly influences the developing identities. Together, children and adults create the atmosphere of the group, and while all are responsible for its development, what the children learn and how the group operates is the responsibility of the adults. It must, however, be recognised that different cultures have different social practices in this respect (Siraj-Blatchford and Clarke, 2000, p26). Language is needed to create a culture, because language is a culturally agreed sign system. It is important for a child to discover that different languages exist, and that, just as s/he can understand others who have different languages, s/he can also be understood by them. Research on multilingualism shows that encountering the different languages spoken in multicultural Europe should be a huge benefit. By taking on and experiencing different roles the child gradually becomes an empathetic and mentally flexible citizen (see Spinthourakis and Sifakis in this volume).

This chapter has shown how a child's social and cultural identity is formed through a process covering every stage of development. It has explored the opportunities for intervention and influence on this process by parents, carers and educators. Cooperation with the child can support the development of identity. There are many influences on the child's identity in a media-rich society, with innovations taking place in nanotechnology and biology, organ transplants and replacements. All these developments may influence identity. Children are growing and creating their own personal memories in this new environment.

5

Rhymes and citizenship: intercultural tools for the kindergarten

Anne-Marie Dinvaut

ost European schools today include pupils from various
cultures. Even the kindergarten school of a small monolingual village will receive echoes of other languages and
other cultures through the media and other social and economic
links with national and global societies. This multicultural environment raises questions about culture and cultures, about the relationship between the individual and these cultures, and about the way an
individual builds his or her identity in different contexts. Adults responsible for children need to work towards the following aims

- to give each child the same learning possibilities, whatever their
  place of birth or cultural roots

- to give groups of children the tools to share cultural and linguistic resources

- to avoid reducing languages and cultures to global and virtual
  products of mass media

- to give pupils elements of genuine human culture.

Rhymes, songs and playground games are often considered as part
of the core of a country's linguistic inheritance. Numerous good col-
lections exist in all parts of the world (Abbis-Chace and Diaz-
Bosetti, 2002; Bustarret, 1986; Favret and Lerasle, 2001; Grosleziat,

2002; Ivanovitch-Lair and Prigent, 2003; Opie and Opie, 1987). This chapter does not collect or classify the rhymes, riddles and songs of various countries, but reflects on two points:

- how can we bring together the enormous possibilities given by these rhymes and by the apprenticeship of shared citizenship?

- how can we extract the core meanings for the development of citizenship from these rhymes and riddles?

Kindergarten teachers often use children's own oral culture to teach the sounds and the structures of the language, as well as to convey aspects of foreign cultures and languages. But there is a risk of reducing this oral culture to its linguistic components and to an archaic folklore, and to omit its role in the building of identity. Some teaching practices might be less positive than they first appear or are intended. For example, when an ethnic minority child who is living in the country in which she was born and attending kindergarten in the same country, is asked by a teacher 'Can you tell us a rhyme from *your* country?' (meaning 'another country'), the child is suddenly identified as being different in some way simply because of her name or skin colour; she is estranged instead of being included and confined by the straitjacket of archaism, exoticism and stereotyping.

Cultural features are never isolated or unconnected but are the components of wide systems of behaviour: children's oral culture is connected with rituals, rules, human relations and ordinary life. This chapter is part of a wider research project (Dinvaut, forthcoming) about the impact of simple classroom resources such as rhymes, songs and riddles on apprenticeship, self-esteem and citizenship.

Learning the sounds of one's language
Rhymes and riddles offer children wonderful tools with which to learn and to share their language. Nonsense syllables and tongue-twisters are particularly effective.

Nonsense syllables

Nonsense syllables in different languages present 'cross-linguistic tendencies', as shown by Arleo (1999); other syllables are not cross-linguistic but specific to their language, they often reproduce the distinctive sounds of their language which allows children to practise these sounds in a playful, poetical and fun way. The few instances given below should encourage teachers to use these nonsense syllables, whatever their language:

In English, [i] and diphthongs:

> *dip, dip, dip*
>
> *miny mo,*

In French, [gr] and [y] :

> *am stram gram*
>
> *turlututu (chapeau pointu).*

In Arabic and English, [i] :

> *eeny, meeny (miny mo) :*
>
> *tita, tita, tita.*

In Spanish, [r]

> *tita tita tariton*

Some rhymes travel across cultures and countries, and then the nonsense syllables become adapted to the new language phonology and written system: so that the British '*Eeny, meeny, miny, mo*' become '*Oh, muni, muni, mei*' in Luxembourg and '*Oh, mini, mini, minimal*' in Germany.

Tongue-twisters

Children also learn sounds through tongue-twisters, which gather similar sounds and trap the speaker into saying peculiar things.

> *Un chasseur sachant chasser, doit savoir chasser sans son chien.*
> [A good hunter can do without his dog]

Louis-Jean Calvet (1984) quotes the following tongue-twister in Fulani, which is the best known of the West African languages, spoken in the sub-Saharan regions from Senegal to Chad: *Nyaamo nyaanya nano, nano nyaanya nyaamo* [the right hand scratches the left one, the left hand scratches the right one]: besides being useful to teach the distinguishing of right and left hands, this tongue-twister can lead the speaker to say *nana* (smell) or *nyaama* (eat) instead of *nyaanya* (scratch).

The educative role of the rhymes

Alone or with playground games, rhymes and songs are tools for teaching attitudes and skills. Every culture possesses songs to teach the child to discover his or her body and to name and move or touch the parts of the body. Here are some of these in German, English, Spanish, French, Wolof, which is the language from near the Senegal River in West Africa:

Brüderlein, komm, tanz mit mir,
beide Hände reich ich dir,
einmal hin, einmal her,
rund herum, das ist nicht schwer.
Mit den Händen, klapp, klapp, klapp
Mit den Füssen, trapp,trapp, trapp
Mit dem Köpfchen, nick, nick, nick
Mit den Fingern, tick, tick, tick

[Young brother, come, dance with me/I give you both hands/to and fro/round and round, it's easy/with the hands/with the feet/ with your small head/with fingers]

Head and shoulders,
Knees and toes (3)
Head and shoulders,
Knees and toes,
Eyes, ears, mouth and nose.

Como planta usted las flores? A la moda, a la moda;
Coma planta usted las flores? A la moda des Paris.
Yo las planto con el dedo, a la moda, a la moda;

58

Yo las planto con el dedo, a la moda de Paris.
(... con las manos, el codo, el pie, etc.)

[How do you plant flowers? In the Paris manner?/ I plant them with my finger, in the Paris manner/ ...with both hands/ ... with one elbow/ ... with one foot...]

Savez-vous planter les choux
à la mode, à la mode –
savez-vous planter les choux
à la mode de chez nous ?
On les plante avec les pieds,
A la mode, à la mode
On les plante avec les pieds,
A la mode de chez nous
Savez-vous....
On les plante avec la main...
On les plante avec le coude...
On les plante avec le nez...

[Can you plant cabbages in our way?/ We plant them with one foot/ ... with both hands/ ... with one elbow/ ... with our nose...]

Tànk, loxo, nopp, bakkan,
Baat, bêt, gémmin, chut!

[Leg, arm, ear, nose/ neck, eyes, mouth, hush! (Children enumerate the seven parts of the body, they follow the rhythm and go quicker and quicker)]

The message conveyed in these rhymes often is: 'your body is your home', and children are first encouraged to name and touch parts of their faces, for they cannot see this part of their bodies. Below are examples of these English, Spanish, French, Italian and Portuguese 'houses':

Knock at the door
Pull the bell,
Lift the latch
And walk in

Una casita muy redondita,
Con dos ventanitas,
Y una puertita,
Y el timbre,
Riiiiiiiiiin!

[A small round house/ with two small windows/ a small door/ and a bell]

Le jardin,
Le trottoir,
Les lumières,
L'escalier,
Les gouttières,
Le grand four.

[The garden/ the pavement/ the lights/ the stairs/ the gutters/ the large oven.]

Jardin poux,
joli front,
nez pointu,
bouche d'argent,
guili guili!

[Nice garden/ nice forehead/ pointed nose/ silver mouth]

Mon toit,
Mon grenier,
Mes deux fenêtres,
Mes deux gouttières,
Mon grand four,
Et mon tambour...
Boum! Boum! Boum!

[My roof/ my attic/ two windows/ two gutters/ a big oven/ and my drum!/ (the child pats her/his stomach)]

Quest'é l'occio bello
Quest'é il suo fratello
Quest'à la chiesina,

Quest'é il campanello che fa
Ding Ding Ding!
O testina blonda
Guancia rubiconda
Bocca sorridente
Fronte innocente

[Here is the nice eye/ here is his brother/ here is the small church/ here is the steeple/ it makes Ding, ding, ding!/ Fair head/ red cheek/ smiling mouth/ innocent forehead]

Tetnho
Janelinha,
Portinha
Campainha, drrr!

Language	Head	Ear	Forehead	Eyes	Nose	Under the nose	Mouth
English	(house)	*Bell*	*door*		*latch*		(door)
Spanish	*Casita*			*ventanitas*	*Timbre* (bell)		*puertita*
French		*Jardin, Toit*	*Grenier* (attic)	*Fenêtres*		*gouttières*	*Argent, Grand four*
Italian					*campanello*		
Portuguese			*Tetnho* (small roof)	*Janelinha,* (small window)	*Campainha, drrr !* (bell)		*Portinha* (small door)

Sometimes the body is symbolised by a homely, familiar object such as the teapot in Britain: *I'm a little tea-pot, short and stout.*

Finger rhymes are often associated with the house (*Here is a house*), to the family and its members (*This family has five people*):

Monsieur Pouce part en voyage.
L'index l'accompagne à la gare,
Le majeur porte la valise,
L'annulaire porte son manteau,
Et le petit auriculaire

61

Qui ne porte rien du tout
Le suit comme un petit toutou.

[Mr Sammy Thumb goes on a journey/ Mr Peter Pointer sees him to the station/ Mr Bobby Big is carrying his case/ Mr Bobby Ring is carrying his coat/ and Tiny Tim/ doesn't do anything/ he follows like a doggie]

En grimpant au plus gros,
J'ai eu mal au dos.
En grimpant au plus pointu,
Je n'ai rien vu.
En grimpant au plus grand,
J'ai perdu mes gants.
En grimpant au plus beau,
J'ai eu trop chaud.
En grimpant au plus petit,
Je me suis dit:
Ça suffit, ça suffit!

[I climbed the biggest one/ and my back was aching;/ I climbed the most pointed one/ and I didn't see anything;/ I climbed the highest one/ and I lost my gloves;/ I climbed the most beautiful one/ and I was too hot;/ I climbed the smallest one/ and I thought:/ that's enough, that's enough!]

In Luxembourg, the fingers live a story that ends well:

Den daimerlek as an de Pëtz gefall
De Féngerlek huet en erausgezunn,
De Laange Baart huet en ofgegréchent,
De Grohänschen huet en an d'Bett geluegt,
An de Stuppschwänzchen huet
Der Mamm et gesot,
dunn huet en eng Botterschmier kritt!

[The thumb fell down the well/ the forefinger dragged him out of it / the middle finger wiped him / the ring finger took him to bed / and the tiny one told his mum everything / and he had bread and butter !

Counting and identifying one's body parts are often combined:

Qui fait un? Moi tout seul!
Qui fait deux? Les oreilles du vieux!
Qui fait trois? Les yeux et le nez!
Qui fait quatre? Les genoux et les coudes!
Qui fait cinq? Les doigts d'une main!
Qui fait six? Les mains, les jambes, les bras!
Qui fait sept? Les trous dans la tête!

[Who's one? I am!/ who's two? The old man's ears!/ Who's three? Eyes and nose!/ Who's four? Elbows and knees!/ Who's five? The fingers of one hand!/ Who's six ? Hands, legs and arms!/ Who's seven? Holes in the head!]

This is not always the case:

Uno dos y tres, pregunta quien es
Cuatro cinco y seis, dice que es el rey
Siete ocho y nueve, abrele si llueve
Diez once y doce, parece que foce
Trece catorce y quince, no vaya a morirse
Dieciseis, diecisiete y dieciocho, el rey del Mapocho
Diecinueve, veinte y veintiuna,
La reina es la Luna
Veintidos, veintitres, veinticuatro,
Està haciendo Teatro
Veinticinco, veintiseis y veintisiete.
Todavia con Chupete
Veintiocho, veintinueve y treinta,
Por ahora se Acabo la cuenta...

[one, two, three, ask who's that?/ four, five, six, the king/ Seven, eight, nine, let him in if it's raining/ Ten, eleven, twelve, isn't he coughing?/ thirteen, fourteen, fifteen, let him live/ Sixteen, seventeen, eighteen, the King of Mapocho/ Nineteen, twenty, twenty-one/ Moon is the Queen/ Twenty-two, twenty-three, twenty-four/ she does some acting/ Twenty five, twenty-six, twenty-seven/ With a lolly/ Twenty-eight, twenty-nine, thirty/ that's enough for today!]

One, two, buckle my shoe;
Three, four, knock at the door;
Five, six, pick up sticks;
Seven eight, lay them straight;
Nine, ten, a good fat hen.
Eleven, twelve, dig and delve;
Thirteen, fourteen, maids a-courting;
Fifteen, sixteen, maids in the kitchen;
Seventeen, eighteen, maids in waiting;
Nineteen, twenty, my plate's empty.

Un nez, deux nez, trois nez,
Quatre nez, cinq nez, six nez.
Sept nez, huit nez, neuf nez
Dînez!

[One nose, two noses, three noses/ four noses, five noses, six noses/ seven noses, eight noses, nine noses/ ten noses! (this has a play on the words 'ten noses', which sounds like 'have dinner']

Un deux trois je m'en vais au bois, etc.
[One, two, three, I go to the wood, ...]

Eins, zwei, Papagei (Germany)
[One, two, parrot...]

Rhymes can teach counting backwards, too: *Ten little Indian boys, Trois petits singes* [Three little monkeys] (Belgium), *Fünf kleine Affen hüpfen auf dem Bett* [Five baby monkeys are jumping on the bed] (Austria).

Games and rhymes often alternate quiet and quick episodes: *La clé de St-Georges* [St Georges's key] (France), *Zakdoek leggen* [Lay the handkerchief] (Denmark), and *Lucy Locket* (Britain) require the children to sing, to be attentive to the person behind them, to anticipate and to react quickly.

Rhymes recall the daily life of the children, and they can encourage children to be brave (*Jack, be nimble*) or to comfort the unfortunate (*Jack and Jill*).

Socialisation

Sharing with others

Children's oral culture socialises them and teaches them how to live together. Beside teaching agility and counting, finger rhymes highlight social skills that are difficult to learn: they acknowledge the fact that sharing is not a natural activity but one that can be very difficult, especially sharing with the youngest brother or sister, as in these examples in German, Spanish, Finish, French and Mina (Ghana and Togo):

Das ist der Daumen
Der schüttelt die Pflaumen
Der sammelt sie auf
Der trâgt sie nach Haus
Und dieser kleine Schelm,
Der iss sie alle alle auf!

[Here is the thumb/ this one shakes the plums down/ this one picks them up/ this one brings them home/ and that little rascal ate them all!]

This little pig went to market
This little pig stayed at home,
This little pig had roast beef,
this little pig had none,
and this little pig cried :
wee wee wee wee
all the way home!

Este compro un huevito
Este lo puso a asar
Este le echo la sal,
Este lo probo un poquito,
Y este picaro gordito...
Se lo comio todo enterito!

[This one bought an egg/ this one cooked it/ this one salted it/ this one tasted it/ and that little rascal ate it all!]

Peulalopotti sai sian, hei
Suomensotti sen kotiin vei
Pitkämies siltä niskat taittoi
Nimeön siitä makkarat laittoi
Sakari pieni sen suuhunsa söi.

[The thumb buys a pig/ the forefinger brings it home/ the middle finger kills it/ the ring finger cooks sausages/ and the tiny one will eat them all!]

Le pouce va à la chasse,
L'index tue un lapin,
Le majeur le fait cuire,
L'annulaire le mange,
Et le petit riquiqui lèche le plat.

[The thumb goes hunting/ the forefinger kills a rabbit/ the middle finger cooks it/ the ring finger eats it/ and the baby one licks the plate]

Eya bé nié nié
Eya bé nukéyé lé wowo
Eya bé ado yé lé wui
Eya bé wo lé wozémé
Eya bé dé mia du
Eya bé dada gbo ma toé né
Déglé fosu sa sakplé !

[This one cries 'wee wee!'/ that one asks 'What's the matter with him!'/ that one says 'he's hungry'/ that one says 'there's flour in the flour box'/ and then 'prepare our dinner!'/ that one says 'I'll tell Mum when she comes back!'/ Thumb is a sneak!]

Respecting rules

Rhymes teach rules and pass on parental messages and guidance; they encourage children to be good, to go to bed earlier and to be polite:

Go to bed late,
Stay very small;

Go to bed early,
Grow very tall.

Un petit chat gris,
Qui mangeait du riz
Sur un tapis gris.
Sa maman lui dit:
'ça n'est pas poli,
de manger du riz,
sur un tapis gris.'

[A grey kitten/ was eating rice/ on a grey carpet/ His mum told him:/ 'That's rude/ to eat rice/ on a grey carpet.']

Rhymes encourage children to be patient when they repeatedly ask the time:

Quelle heure est-il ?
L'heure perdue,
la bête la cherche,
Comme hier à la même heure.
La même heure que demain à la même heure.

[What's the time? Time you knew better. What's the time? A minute to the next. What's the time? about now. What's the time? the same time as it was this time yesterday.]

Children's society has its own rules and its oral culture conveys regulatory messages. Children's rhymes are texts to guarantee sincerity, to conclude a treaty, to obtain respite in a game, to choose, and to select or to eliminate a player. Iona and Peter Opie (1986) collected these rhymes under the title of *A Code of Oral Legislation,* and Andy Arleo (2003) stresses that this 'legal folklore' allows direct peer transmission of the rules of language and the rules of life. A very well known example is the dipping rhyme. Here are dipping rhymes from Great Britain and Rwanda:

One potato, two potatoes, three potatoes, four
Five potatoes, six potatoes, seven potatoes, more.
O-U-T spells out.

Eeny, meeny, miny mo...
Dip, dip, dip, my blue ship...

Kabuye kanjye
Kabuye kanjye ni keza pe (2)
Enda nawe ukarore,
nawe ukarore
ni keza pe.

[My little stone/ is very nice/ Take it, have a look/ have look/ it is so nice!]

Transgressing rules

Wise governments should listen to rhymes. These ancient tools show that a little transgression, humour and creativity can create the breathing space which allows respect for the rules. Rhymes are very efficient tools for teaching the language but they also convey techniques of transgressing linguistic rules and invite children to play at nonsense: the ship is sailing like a cup and saucer; you can catch the tiger's toe; if you dip a mouse into oil it becomes a snail.

Dip, dip, dip
My blue ship
Sails on the water
Like a cup and saucer.
You're not on

Eeeny, meeny, miny, mo,
Catch a tiger by his toe.
If he squeals, let him go.
Eeeny, meeny, miny, mo.

Une souris verte, qui courait dans l'herbe
Je l'attrape par la queue,
Je la montre à ces Messieurs,
Ces Messieurs me disent:
'Trempez-la dans l'huile,
Trempez-la dans l'eau,
Ça fera un escargot tout chaud'

[A green mouse was running on the grass/ I catch it by its tail/ I show it to the lords/ They tell me/ 'Dip it into oil/ dip it into water/ to make it a hot snail']

School is a place where rules are taught and transgressed. The song below was collected in 1998 during a school exchange: Italian children were teaching it to their new British, French and German friends. Their Italian teachers had never heard this truancy song before:

Siamo studenti,
Siamo una massa di deficenti.
Non ci piace l'italiano,
Ma ci piace Celentano.
Basta la storia, la geografia,
Forza regarzi andiamo via.
Salutiamo la maestra
Con la scusa del mal di testa,
Salutiamo il professore
Con la scusa del raffreddore,
Salutiamo la supplente
Con la scusa del mal di dente,
Salutiamo il direttore
Con la scusa del mal di cuore.

[We are pupils/ all of us are sick/ We don't like Italian/ we prefer Celentano/ We're fed up with History and Geography/ we want to go/ Bye-bye teacher/ we have a head ache/ bye-bye teacher/ we caught a cold/ bye-bye assistant/ we have tooth ache / bye-bye head-master/ we feel dizzy]

The taming of the aggressive and mocking self

Children's oral culture recognises that aggressive feelings cannot be avoided. Rhymes channel these aggressive tendencies: the use of a set form of words can calm the children down and the ritual can deter them from violence. Mocking rhymes teach children that they will have to cope with others' mockery and makes them conscious that that mockery is a long-standing human trait. Mocking rhymes can depersonalise and lighten the act of mocking. This message is conveyed by the following spitting jokes in German, English, French or Khmer, which is spoken in Cambodia, Thailand, Vietnam: (**bold type** indicates the spitting episode),

Ich sage dir wahr, deine Hand ist klar. Ich sage dir was, deine Hand ist nass.
[I tell you the truth, your hand is clean. I tell you what, **your hand is dirty**] (Böhme, cited by Opie, p63)

*Here's where the barn is, and here's where the cowshed is. And here in the middle, is the **duck pond***

*Je vais lire ton avenir... oh, tu seras très riche. Tu auras une grande maison, dans un grand parc. Et même, au milieu, **une piscine!***
[I will read your destiny: you will become a rich man. You will have a big mansion, with a large park. In the park, you will even have a **swimming-pool**] (collected in Lyon, France, 1995)

*Je verse l'eau d'une noix de coco, j'attrape la queue du poisson Saa, je cache un coquillage dans ma poche, mais toi, prends bien garde à tes cheveux, **un oiseau va faire caca juste au milieu!***
[*Translation, from Ivanovitch-Lair and Prigent, 2003*]

This social apprenticeship is connected with the learning of language and its tricks.

Une oie,
Deux oies,
Trois oies,
Quatre oies,
Cinq oies,
Six oies,
c'est toi!

[One goose/ two geese/ three geese/ four geese/ five geese/ six geese/ seven geese (which sounds like 'this [goose] is you!')]

Being witty

Rhymes not only teach the language: they train the child not to get caught out by the language itself, and they advise the child not to be too credulous.

Look, there's something on your tongue (the person puts out his tongue). *Good dog!* (Opie, 1986).

T'as une tache (the person pokes her/his head forward, the other snaps at her/his nose)

Moustache!

[you've got a spot (on your shirt)]

In Spain, France, Britain and the Netherlands, the following rhymes teach that one should think before answering. These four pinching rhymes are similar, if the child concentrates too much on remembering and answering them and forgets the double meanings, s/he gets caught:

*Juan y **Pinchame***
Fueron a nadar.
Juan se ahogo
Quien quedo?
'Pinchame!'
'Ay!'

*Pince-mi et **Pince-moi***
Sont dans un bateau
Pince-mi tombe à l'eau,
Qu'est-ce qui reste?

*Adam and Eve and **Pinch-me***
Went down to the river to bathe
Adam and Eve were drowned
Who do you think was saved?

*Knijp-me-eens en **Krab-me-eens***
Die zaten in een bootje;

Knijp-me-ens die viel er uit,
Wie bleef er toeng nog over?
(Netherlands, collected by Opie, p60)

Language games teach children not to answer mechanically and to remain attentive. These self-incriminating traps require children to modify their answer several times:

I went up one pair of stairs
– Just like me
I went up two pairs of stairs
– Just like me
I opened the door
– Just like me
I crossed the room
– Just like me
I looked out of the window
– Just like me
And saw a monkey
*– **Just like me***
(Opie, 1986)

I am a gold lock
– I am a gold key
I am a silver lock
– I am a silver key
I am a brass lock
– I am a brass key
I am a monk lock
*– **I am a monkey***
(Opie, 1986)

Il passe une voiture, qu'y a-t-il dedans? Un panier
Qu'y a-t-il dans le panier? De la paille.
Qu'y a-t-il dans la paille? Une poule.
Qu'y a-t-il sous la poule? Un œuf.
Qu'y a-t-il dans le blanc? Le jaune.
Qu'y a-t-il dans le jaune? Une aiguille.

Qu'y a-t-il dans l'aiguille? Un trou.
Qu'y a-t-il dans le trou? Une grosse bête qui court après toi !

[Here is a car. What's in it? A basket/ What's in the basket?
Straw/ What's on the straw? A hen/ What's under the hen? An
egg/ What's in the white? The yolk/ What's in the yolk? A
needle/ What's in the needle? An eye/ What's in the eye (in
French, 'hole')?/ What's in the hole? A big animal that chases
you!] (Switzerland, collected by Ivanovitch-Lair and Prigent,
2003)

From a linguistic point of view these self-incrimination traps are
perfect drills. They are humorous, they contribute to socialisation,
and they have a goal. They thus are a great contrast to the dull and
inefficient repeated practice that is still frequent during foreign language lessons.

Being sensible
Riddles invite children to trust their reasoning more than their
preconceptions in these examples from Britain and France:

Which is heavier, a pound of feathers or a pound of lead?
(Opie, 1986)

*Qu'est-ce qui est le plus lourd, un kilo de plumes ou un kilo de
plomb?*

Rhymes as a mirror
Rhymes and songs can express concerns from children's lives, from
small worries to big anxieties. To get to sleep, the child checks that
all the members of the family are here:

Fais dodo, Colas, mon p'tit frère,
Fais dodo, t'auras du lolo.
Maman est en haut,
Qui fait des gâteaux,
Papa est en bas,
Fait du chocolat.
Fais dodo.

[Hush, baby, go to sleep/ you will have milk/ Mum is upstairs/ and cooking cakes/ Dad is downstairs/ and cooking chocolate/...]

Rhymes can evoke some adult absurdities:

Mother, may I go out to bathe?
Yes, my darling daughter.
Hang your clothes on yonder tree,
But don't go near the water!

Some rhymes can be chosen for the wider message they give about life, such as this Arabic rhyme from the Maghreb:

Achmisa ana na'tik sannat lahmar
Oua'tini sannat laghzal.
[O sun! I give you a donkey tooth/ give me a gazelle tooth]

Hafida Favret and Magdeleine Lerasle (2001) explain that when children loose baby teeth in the Maghreb, they offer them to nature with this rhyme. They throw them into the sea, into the sky or the sun, or they bury them. This pre-Muslim saying can be heard in Algeria, Tunisia and Morocco: it symbolises life's generosity and comforts the child by assuming that whenever something is lost life will offer something better. The Arabic world considers the gazelle to be the most beautiful thing on earth. When one door closes, another one opens.

Conclusion

Constantin von Barloewen's analysis of globalisation (2003) can be applied to kindergarten schools: he compares cultures using the tools of anthropology and concludes that the dialogue between cultures is the only solution to conflicts. He argues that this dialogue should lead neither to a sole universal culture which is above all others, nor to multiculturality as a patchwork of different and unconnected cultures. It should lead to *interculturality*: being able to communicate, to acknowledge the other and to consider one's culture as relative to others: 'Interculturality is more than the combination of one's culture and of the foreign culture. It arises a new appreciation of oneself, which rises from both the consciousness of the relativism of values and the universality of human culture' (Von Barloewen, 2003, p346).

In kindergarten schools, careful choice of cultural tools can contribute to building interculturality among a group of children and allow them to build their own identity and to understand universality (see Maggie Ross in this volume). The rhymes selected can help teachers to avoid archaisms and stereotypes and they can use them as tools to support diversity. This will show children from different cultures that they share many similar values. Rhymes allow children to acknowledge individual cultures through activities designed for all children. No child is identified as a 'stranger', and all children contribute to the development of a common interculture and of harmonious citizenship. Allowing children to transmit this ancient and vivid oral culture in the playground, as they have always done, without interference, is of enormous value.

6

Young children's identities and first experiences of democracy

Yveline Fumat

his chapter is concerned with two aspects of early years educational provision which have an interdependent relationship. First, the transition of the young child from the family to the school or a caring institution must be carried out with immense care and sensitivity for the child's developing identity. Second and linked to this, we must consider how early years settings are concerned with aspects of education for democracy, in particular the young child's feeling of belonging and of how to learn, understand and follow rules. The chapter asks 'which types of education and learning process favour the development of 'democratic personalities' in institutions during the early years?' Although this is an early stage for citizenship education, do children have experiences at this age which will prepare them for citizenship in a democratic society?

'Civic behaviour' and 'living together' are the premises and foundations of citizenship education. Children's *identities*, their relationships to others and their participation in a group are at stake. In a democratic society, children's socialisation involves supporting their *individualisation*, their autonomy and their social participation. Democratic societies aim to develop individual creativity and critical thinking. The socialisation process in a democratic society – and *for* a democratic society – assumes specific features that must be asserted at each stage of children's secondary socialisation.

The point of arrival

When young children first arrive at an institution it is important to ensure that they are not overwhelmed by the group they join and that they do not feel 'lost' or unsafe in the group. The transition from the familiar to a new environment can be achieved more steadily when a secure relationship has already been established between child and mother (Ainsworth *et al*, 1978; Ainsworth, 1991). Nevertheless, the institution is responsible for being attentive to children's difficulties and needs to consider these with care.

First, educators must imagine what the separation from a smaller, cosy environment, dominated by affectionate relationships implies for children. They must imagine how children may experience loss and a feeling of exile. The child is taken away from her or his family and may feel alone in a complex and vast new space. Children are expected to take part in new activities, the purpose of which they may not initially understand. They must rely on adults whom they hardly recognise, and face groups whose size and strength can be threatening. They have the feeling of facing a 'multitude' (both in terms of numbers and of undifferentiability). The feeling of exile experienced by adults when they arrive in a new institution, such as a hospital, may help us to understand young children's feelings:

> I don't really know where I am, what is going to happen to me, what I am supposed to do, who are these people looking after me, but still I know that I am in an institution which cares for me! I am going to be far from my loved ones, from my familiar habits,... first, I am going to close myself up, turn to the only personal things I have left, some clothes, some objects, some memories....

Those children who have not yet developed an inner world and are not confident that this is all for their own good may feel even more helpless.

The institution' staff needs to imagine the child's perception of rupture and to ease the necessary transition by:

* offering visits with parents and carers prior to the first day of attendance

- marking out spaces with suitable colours and logos for children who can not read, making visible paths towards the toilets and rooms with specific purposes

- creating refuge corners, which are rest spaces where they won't feel the pressure of the group to such an extent

- introducing time rituals which are signalled by gestures and signals

Nothing is obvious to the young child. Easily identifiable markers are a way to protect her or his sense of feeling safe and to avoid feelings of abandonment, as well as providing a pathway through a complex institution where they will change status and grow up.

Initially the institution must ensure that the child does not feel overwhelmed by the group and that new and trusting relationships are established within it. It is absolutely essential to recognise children's individual identities. Young children may need to be called, both orally and in writing, by their first and last names. The last name alone is not enough (we need to distinguish each child from brothers and sisters), nor is the first name by itself enough (we need to distinguish each child from other children with the same first name). When arriving in this new place for the first time children must be given their full civic identity, rather than 'babyish' nicknames which may have been used before.

Rituals can be used to encourage integration into the group. For example, the child could hand in a paper with their first and last names written on it. This might mean that they accept the community by demonstrating that they want to be part of it and that they are recognised as named and individualised persons. This action would lose its symbolic dimension if the paper is handed in by the mother.

The welcome to the nursery

Welcoming a two or three year-old into a nursery may involve radically challenging the expectations and mental pictures of a nursery worker who is accustomed to working with older children. How can the worker's view of a two year-old infant be positive, if her expectations are based on experience of the skills of a three to four year-old? This is even more marked if the institution does not take account of individual needs and only allows children to express themselves in terms of deviance or passivity. For example, a two year-old child might be recorded as follow:

> In a group, s/he is agitated... when involved in physical activities, she remains on the side lines or is pushed about by the older ones and wants her security blanket. When expected to behave like others, s/he does not quite follow what is going on and when s/he is not invited to join in, s/he wants to emulate the bigger ones and hampers the serious activity... S/he doesn't even know how to draw a circle and remains impervious to the slightest collective instruction.

From such a perspective s/he can only assume the status of 'bad boy/girl' or trouble-maker, unless her apparent passivity helps her to become invisible and consequently s/he does not disturb others in the group. To view an infant as one would view an older child is discriminatory and will frustrate the adult and demean the child.

How should such a child's self-esteem and self-confidence be restored and reinforced? In the best scenario, a child who is not showing sufficient signs of maturity would be described as not yet being ready for school: it should be evident that the child is being asked to adapt to the school, rather than the school adapting itself to the needs of the child. What could be more unsettling for a child than to arrive in an unknown place and to be surrounded by people whom s/he has never seen before in her or his life? An appropriate welcome to the nursery will help new arrivals to familiarise themselves gradually with the school and to anticipate what they are about to experience.

Nevertheless, no matter how well the first day in nursery is organised, the child may demonstrate, through body-language or through attitudes, her or his difficulty in making the separation from her/his carer and in accepting the rules of the new setting. Although s/he has been undergoing a process of separation and individuation since birth, her/his sense of self will still be very fragile. S/he can act out insecurities in many ways: hiding in her/his shell, regressing, being defensively aggressive or being hyperactive. Sometimes, her/his extreme distress will manifest itself through violent or silent tears. Some psychopathological symptoms may develop: regression in potty training which may have been only recently mastered, biting, inhibitions or extreme shyness. It is therefore important not to identify the child with her/his symptom by calling her/ him 'naughty' or 'dirty' and not to show aggression to the child, as this only has the effect of increasing her/his feelings of insecurity.

For the teacher or nursery worker the difficulty lies in distinguishing between insecurities which may pass and those which may be more permanent and may require later attention. Gradually settling the child in, with the help of a caring adult, will make the child feel valued, but it may be necessary to review the school's policies by allowing the carer to stay in the classroom for a while, or by reducing the length of child's day in school.

The two year-old requires greater vigilance both because of his/her immaturity and her/his close relationship with his/her family. His/her dependence on this relationship is important not only in meeting her/his physiological needs but also at affective and cognitive levels. S/he needs this particular relationship with a significant adult to find her/his boundaries and to be reassured. The teacher or early years worker can, through her interactions, help him/her with the mental elaboration of separation from this adult. The teacher or nursery worker should not be a mother substitute, which might make her a rival, but should take on a transitional role. The young child needs her/his mother to look at him/ her, talk to her/him and help him/her make sense of what s/he is going through, what s/he is doing, and to reaffirm her/his narcissism and self-esteem. All this can only happen if s/he is positively and unconditionally recognised as her/his parents' child.

Taking very young children through these early steps of integration at school is difficult for adults: it requires them not only to think about and to organise the first day in nursery so that it goes well but it also makes great emotional demands on the adult, to welcome each child and her/his parents. Such emotive resonances can lead to reactions that are detrimental: there is a risk of adopting either an impulsive or rigid attitude or one of emotional disengagement in order to protect oneself, and not choosing to see the child's distress. The teacher is required to act without being discouraged, impatient or resentful. Managing these internal conflicts and dealing with the child's opposition or distress which is caused by separation can be destabilising: hard 'emotional labour'. For the teacher there is no such thing as a 'proper' attitude.

It is well-recognised that working with children requires a great deal of patience. This is true both because trust is required in children and their capability to grow and develop and they need to be given time to find their boundaries and overcome the transitional difficulties. The adult has to be both aware and spontaneous: this requires a conscious effort to distance oneself from the situation, which depends on a supportive working team and continuing professional development.

A professional relationship with parents

The younger the child, the stronger the potential for a perception of rivalry between her significant adult and the teacher. Being aware of the potential complexity of the situation enables the professional to recognise the difficulties of both the parent and the child, and to sensitively separate them and avoid projecting value judgments which can be latent sources of conflict with the family.

For example, one mother seems in a hurry to leave her child in the nursery, whilst another appears to wait until hers cries before she leaves and prolongs her goodbyes: both demonstrate that they have difficulty in separating, and this needs to be approached by the professional with tact and firmness. If an aggressive reaction by the child is interpreted as an attempt to express feelings of uneasiness, and not as directed personally at the teacher, it can open up channels for more trusting communication.

In France the nursery is both a free child-minding service and a school, so the teacher is also confronted with some paradoxical situations. She may wish to set up an individual programme for each child, to enabling him to settle into the rhythm of the school without difficulties. However, the reality of the child's parents being unavailable because they are working does not easily allow for such transition. Difficulties in settling can help set up the comparison between the 'good professional' and the 'bad parent'. The teacher may declare that the parents have 'given up'. But this kind of abusive value judgment is more likely to be a defensive position, rather than the attitude of a professional who listens respectfully to the parents.

Family relationships are emotional and irrational: professional relationships with children and their parents should be dispassionate, allowing each child to adapt, and allowing the educator to be attentive to the needs of both children and parents. How can this be done in a fair way, unobstructed by preconceptions? Some suggestions may be helpful:

- be reassuring to parents, particularly by making positive observations about their child and by allowing them to reassure their child

- respect the child's transitional objects such as security blankets, dummies or photographs

- organise communication with the family about what is learnt in school, by using photo albums and 'my life' notebooks, which are described below. This will build coherence between the different areas of the child's life so that the passage from family to school is seen as progress, not as abandonment or abduction.

Communication between teachers and families is key to the schooling system. Activities in school acquire more meaning for the child when they also have meaning for their parents. Welcoming parents who may have ambivalent feelings about school and supporting their parental position means the professional must step back, listen and have the confidence to accept this view.

Finally, the notion of a contract with the family can be established by setting up a personal project for each child that sets milestones along the way. This will ensure better integration, allowing exceptions to be made by the nursery workers and giving parents the chance to be involved. The parents will then be seen as genuine school/nursery partners

Developing a feeling of belonging and partnership

Once a child is introduced into the nursery setting, s/he need to feel that s/he belongs to the group. These will arise from being together, and by getting involved in common activities. But we must distinguish different kinds of activity.

Activities in unison

Singing, dancing and speaking in chorus are all activities that allow children to be part of a group and are important socialisation skills. However, these activities should not become the main or only way of 'being with others'. This may lead to the child becoming over-dependent on the group relationship. It is necessary to distinguish between socialisation process that are aimed at absorbing the individual into the group, in which s/he will lose her/his identity as an individual, and those where the ultimate aim is the autonomy (*auto nomos*) of individuals. Children also need to be socialised to be sufficiently independent to follow their own laws (exercising moral responsibility) and to build a political society in which law is desired by all (the 'social contract' of democratic societies).

Activities such as singing together, walking together, or reciting the verses of a sacred text together are good tools for those integrated and holistic societies in which the common good prevails over the needs of the individual (Dumont, 1980, 1985). But the ideal of a democratic society is also that individuals learn to govern themselves, controlling their urges through moral law, constructing common rules for living together and building the laws of the *civitas*. In democratic societies, individuals must act alone, think alone, and learn to make their own choices.

Cooperative activities

Group activities that involve differentiated roles will contribute towards developing integration and individualisation. These are activities in which each person is given a place, or a role to play, or a contribution to make: these activities will increase children's self consciousness and their consciousness of other people's roles. Collective work, such as painting a fresco or a model together, precedes the construction, through the participation of all in the political *civitas*. Being recognised by others through these activities increases self-esteem. Group activities help to develop an understanding of the 'rules of the game'.

Children arrive in the educational institution after their primary socialisation within the family, where they were largely still in a close relationship with their mother (see Korhonen and Helenius in this volume). The new institution begins to separate them from this close relationship and contributes to their growth and to their departure from the family cocoon.

Françoise Dolto (1995) warns against reproducing a dependency on the group which only contributes to deepening the fusional relationship with the mother. Some children who appear quiet, shy and immature when entering the institution will closely imitate older children. They will not take the initiative and will become accustomed to following others, submitting to others and stepping aside. The delay in the socialisation process increases because of this 'carrier group' effect, and this may pass unnoticed since these children are not disruptive or undisciplined.

A tool for partnership: a 'life notebook'

The idea of a life notebook is to bring home to school and school to home. The life notebook is unique to each child and is a way to express the link between family life and school activities. It represents a transitional dimension between the family micro-culture and the school culture. The notebook is used to record the child's activities and experiences in school and at home, and becomes a significant network between the two. As a witness to the child's life it records the child's memories and has a strong emotive value.

The object of the life notebook is to be a communication development project with the child at the centre:

- to ease the welcoming of each child into school and to maintain links with his/her family

- to suggest useful socialising activities so that everyone feels recognised and is encouraged to maintain progress

- to attach importance to situations where communication takes place, which enables dialogue between parents and teachers and encourages reading the book.

As the child regularly brings home her/his life notebook, the parents, through their child, have the opportunity to become more sensitive and engage with the project. The notebook involves them in the learning process and in using narrative skills.

The child sees adults reading his/her life notebook, which enables her/him to construct a model of a reader and to observe the postures, attitudes and strategies of the reader. From a very young age, s/he will understand when and why to use one's writing skills.

Learning to follow the rules
The regulation of children's exchanges begins very early. As soon as children have physical contact they are capable of 'acting dialogues' (Bruner, 1990, 1996): exchanging, cooperating and even negotiating, accepting giving up an object, offering it in order to appease. At a very early stage babies know, often without the intervention of an adult, how to solve their conflicts and how to set up rules for cooperation. Nurseries are not only made of cries and violence, and young children are not only competitors and rivals. Expressions of solicitude are more frequent than we think: young children know how to comfort and how to empathise with another who is crying. If we perceive nurseries as a jungle, we will tend to separate children and watch over them, because of fear of the risks and dangers of fighting. Research in Hungary by Emmi Pikler (1994) and in France by CRESAS (2004) suggests that peaceful exchanges can take place, but only if children have a free rein and adult intervention is not constant and constraining. If all children's activities are programmed, if all objects are formatted for 'educational purposes' and no real space of exploration is possible, then the rules of the game

cannot be built: to construct these, genuine experience of peer communication is essential.

Nevertheless, not all rules can be established by the children themselves, and they will need to learn institutional rules. Rules against incest and violence are found in all societies: what psychoanalysis calls 'the Law'. Respect for these laws gives us our humanity and allows access to a symbolic discourse through exchange and speech. This primordial law can not be challenged, since it is precisely the basis for language and discussion.

All other rules change over historical time. Their content is likely to vary depending on contexts. Helping children to understand the value and importance of rules, in situations tailored for them, is essential. They must understand that laws are created by men and women. The way they obey the law and contribute to the establishment of new laws depends on this initial understanding. Citizenship education does not begin by a detailed learning of the laws of one's own country, but by a deep understanding of what laws are for. During the early years laws may be understood as absolute on the basis of limited experiences which are nonetheless real: this is neither reverence nor deference. Democracy is not only about citizens complying with the law: it also about citizens being willing to change the law.

In conclusion, the first experiences of young children when they are separated from their family may be of citizenship. But only if we ensure they understand they are recognised to same extent as others, that they are fairly treated, and that their participation in the peer group and the institution is not detrimental to their own freedom, but rather opens more possibilities for action and gives them more power to exert themselves on the surrounding environment. Secondary socialisation is not only a matter of 'respecting' individuality, it is also about supporting the development of individuality, through structures and through pedagogical practices. This is the only educational project compatible with democratic ideals.

7

Children's intercultural identity development through the teaching of languages

Julia A. Spinthourakis and Nicos Sifakis

The notion of identity is a complicated one. It is a psychosocial terrain where different aspects of an individual's *persona* meet to shape his or her attitudes and beliefs. Throughout the development of our life, elements of intelligence, mind, personality, and self work together to create our identity (Demetriou, 2003). This process is continuous throughout life, but it is more crucial in childhood. In this chapter we consider the links between identity, intercultural identity and competence with language and communication. We focus on the teaching, learning and use of foreign languages as a mechanism to enhance identity and as a means of leading to a child's intercultural competence. We conclude with some thoughts about foreign language teacher training.

Identity and language

The links between identity and language have been numerous and widely debated in the relevant literature (for a comprehensive review, see Blackledge and Pavlenko, 2001). According to one perspective, language is the means of *expressing* one's identity, providing 'facts about their class, sex, age, and region' (Chambers, 1995, pp 100-101). These expressions of identity are claimed to be 'common knowledge' that is shared by all and creates certain expectations about who individual people are on the basis of 'how they sound'.

This viewpoint has been severely criticised by sociolinguists who claim that identity is not a fixed but a dynamic notion. They emphasise the possibility of a single identity performing different functions and of the existence of multiple identities in the same person (Johnstone, 1996). As a result, identity is the result of a series of *negotiation* processes between the agent and her/his environment, which means that more attention should be paid to local and constructed, rather than to expressed, aspects of identity (Lo, 1999).

The negotiation process is at the heart of other related definitions of identity. Thus, according to Tajfel (1981), social identity is based on the notion of 'group membership'. This negotiation is seen as an active process, in which individuals attempt to evoke, assert, define, modify, challenge and/or support their own and others' desired self-images (Ting-Toomey, 1999, p40). Identity is viewed as reflective self-images constructed, experienced, and communicated by individuals within a culture and within the context of a particular interaction (Ting-Toomey, 1999, p39). In this sense, culture is inextricably linked with language: it is perceived as 'a pattern of learned, group-related perceptions – including both verbal and non-verbal language, attitudes, values, belief systems, disbelief systems, and behaviours – that is accepted and expected by an identity group' (Singer, 1998, p96).

It should be stressed that this notion of culture adopts a more 'personalised' viewpoint, along the lines of Holliday (1999), and extends from each individual's specific beliefs and actions (that are under his/her conscious control) to the prescribed ethnic, national and international sense of 'culture' (which is not consciously controlled individually). Holliday's perspective of 'small' cultures helps avoid stereotyping and approaches each communicative situation as a single cultural 'event'.

More expansive accounts of identity have focused on the fact that identity is a more complicated construct that should be also be linked with accounts concerning the social, cultural, gender-related, economic, and generational stratification characteristics of all societies. In the post-structuralist domain, different ethnographically-oriented socio-linguistic approaches emphasise the role of language in the construction of identity. This contrasts with Bourdieu's (1991) view of language as a form of symbolic capital and Weedon's (1987) view of language as a site of identity construction. Within this framework, Blackledge and Pavlenko view identity 'as the study of linguistic ideology as a bridge between linguistic and social theory, linking considerations of language use, attitudes and beliefs with considerations of power and social inequality' (2001, p253).

Identity formation in children
It follows that some processes of identity formation are even more important in childhood. Language plays a key role as the main tool children use to get to know the world around them (Rampton, 1995). As a result, communication through language and the various linguistic and non-linguistic mechanisms of discourse, discussed below, is especially important. As the main element of the negotiation process, language communication is not only the route to children's development of literacy (Burnett and Myers, 2002) but the means by which young children engage in the creation of their own decision-making mechanisms (Byrnes, 1998), a process that both subtle and invaluable for the rest of their lives (Howse, Best and Stone, 2003).

The so-called 'socialisation agents such as parents, siblings, teachers, and the media' are of definitive importance in these processes (Rosenfield and Stephan, 1981, p274; Katsillis and Rubinson, 1990). The family environment plays a central role in the development of children's identity (Spinthourakis and Katsillis, 2004), but friends are of equal importance (Erwin, 1985) and so are peers (Ryan, 2001).

Intercultural identity and language
We have seen that identity is not a static, fixed and inactive whole but a dynamic and flexible, and to a large extent consciously controlled, state of becoming. This is also true for intercultural identity, which, in its simplest form, involves the associating of an individual's own socio-cultural identity with that (or those) of another (or

others). In the same way, by 'intercultural', we mean the 'contextual, heuristic, and comparative dimensions' that orient different individuals to 'the idea of culture as difference, especially as difference in the realm of group identity' (Appadurai, 1996, p13).

There are different descriptive perspectives of the process of intercultural development. The theory of *acculturation* projects an overly linear trajectory from culture A to culture B. The theory of *syncretism* describes the two (or more) cultural systems in a clearly overlaying fashion. These two quite simplistic accounts are thrown into contrast by the theory of *contact zones*, which 'suggests a dyadic relationship and a mutual entanglement of cultural practices and modes of representing cultural identity with disputes and struggles over interpretative power' (Singh and Doherty, 2004, p12). In these contact zones, individuals 'meet, clash, and grapple with each other, often in highly asymmetrical relations of domination and subordination' (Pratt, 1992, p4). This negotiation process clearly involves expressing one's own identity through communicating and being exposed to whatever one can take in from such an encounter. The resulting identity, which is itself in constant flux, can be called intercultural, to the extent that it involves the making and remaking of one's identity along the intercultural frontiers of peoples and nations (Pratt, 2002).

It is interesting to see the links between identity, and particularly intercultural identity, with citizenship. Byram (1998), in his discussion of the notion of citizenship, mentions that this is achieved in various ways and stresses the importance of education. It is primarily the responsibility of the state, and 'is usually done in courses of education for citizenship or civic education and/or by involving learners in the politics of the school as an entity' (p349). If citizenship is perceived as 'the simple transmission of knowledge and skills' that is meant to reinforce a sense of national identity, then it is not connected to language issues as such. But if citizenship is perceived as one of the ultimate aims of education, whose main purpose should be to develop 'critical citizens', then language issues play a central role. They delineate a framework for the 'different voices and traditions [that] exist and flourish' in a country (Giroux, 1992, p134) and they are a means of considering the extent to which everyone's voices are heard in the community. An example of how the notion of intercultural identity can enhance people's notion of citizenship beyond the level of the single nation-state is the advent of the euro in the European Union (Risse, 2003). With the introduction of the euro, Euroland citizens' identification with the EU and Europe in general has been significantly promoted – despite different reactions by different nation-states.

Language and communication

We have seen that language plays a key role in the formation of identity. But what do we mean by language? This is a difficult question to answer, but an important one, especially as it concerns intercultural identity. In its simplest sense, language can be defined as a 'system' of arbitrary symbols used for human communication (Hatch, 1992). Such communication can be either transactional or interactional (Brown and Yule, 1983). It is transactional when it prioritises communication of a particular message, such as carrying out a bank transaction or ordering a meal at a restaurant. It is interactional when it is concerned with the expression of one's attitudes and the establishment of social relations, as in chatting about the weather at the bus stop or talking with friends at a dinner party.

However, there is more to communication than this. For all interactional and transactional messages to be effective – that is, successfully interpreted by others – they must conform to the criteria of correctness, appropriacy and effectiveness (Canale and Swain, 1980; Canale, 1983). Correctness means the capability of the communicator to express her or his thoughts without ambiguity, with enough structural accuracy and functional fluency to meet the needs of each communicative exchange (see Brumfit, 1984; Hamersley, 1991). Appropriacy refers to elements of discourse that make communication socially and culturally 'acceptable' by other participants at each moment: these issues are studied in pragmatics (as in Mey, 2001 or Bredella, 2003). Effectiveness means that the discourse must be intelligible, or comprehensible, to other participants.

These different aspects of communication are essential ingredients of all successful interactions and transactions. Together, they form different levels of communicative capability, or competence, that communicators should possess (Canale and Swain, 1980). Thus we can refer to a 'discourse competence', which refers to communicators' knowledge of the rules governing 'the combination of utterances and communicative functions' in language use (*ibid*), a 'linguistic competence', referring to the mastery of the general rules of language as abstracted from its use, and a 'pragmatic competence', which concerns the ability to communicate appropriately in particular contexts. Furthermore, 'strategic competence' enables participants to cope with problematic communicative situations and to keep communication open, whereas 'intercultural competence' concerns the participants' sense of belonging to a particular identity group and its corresponding culture (Singer, 1998 – see above).

Intercultural identity is seen to be inextricably bound up with all aspects of communication. It is therefore impossible to carry out transactions or interactions with others without engaging and exhibiting, to a greater or lesser extent, our intercultural identity. What is more, it is essential for all communicators to be aware of the effects their discourse will have on their interlocutors, especially if the latter come from a different socio-cultural background. According to Hymes (1974), such an awareness involves knowledge of the physical 'setting' and psychological 'scene' of each communicative situation, which is the culturally-specific system for reference to time and space in the particular culture. It also requires an understanding of who is involved in the transaction, or who addresses what to whom, and each participant's social roles and status. Knowing the purpose of the communication is also important, as it helps to monitor the purposes of what we want to say and the outcomes of the communication. Such an awareness will determine the form of the message (for example, whether to use the active or passive voice), and the paralinguistic or non-verbal 'tone, manner, or spirit' of the way a communicative event is performed (Hymes, 1974, p57).

Every communicative event should be understood with reference to the social and cultural norms which govern it and which account for the participants' actions and reactions. These norms essentially define what is and what is not appropriate or expected. The rules of conversational turn-taking are an example of this. In this sense, Hymes' categories are a very productive and powerful tool for making sense of the textual, situational and socio-cultural characteristics of each communicative event (Brown and Yule, 1983; Sifianou, 2001).

Foreign language education and intercultural competence

The issue of identity development and the demands of intercultural competence have always been central concerns in foreign language teaching. Pedagogues have frequently referred to Hymes' categories as a means of characterising both general as well as more specific aspects of all communicative events. For example, the general aspects may refer to the participants' role and status, their choice of formal or informal discourse or their attitudes, emotions, inferencing procedures, cultural and world knowledge and perception of the communicative situation. On the other hand, the specific aspects may refer to their gestures and paralinguistic features (such as the tone of voice, facial characteristics, speed of delivery, and so on). These analyses have helped teachers' understanding of both language uses and language users in different individual communicative situations. They have also made them appreciate the complicatedness of communicating, which, according to some foreign language researchers, demands an equally complicated and multifaceted competence (see Cook, 1991).

The importance of foreign languages to younger learners, especially learning English as a second or foreign language (Day, 2002 – also see below) has been emphasised. Extensive research has shown that children have an advantage over adults in their ability to learn language (Mayo, del Pilar and Lecumberri, 2003), which has prompted educational institutions around the world to use foreign language teaching to promote intercultural learning at primary school (for a recent review, see Guilherme, 2002; also Sercu, 2002).

95

Teachers can do many things to help promote learners' intercultural competence. If the foreign language classroom is multilingual, i.e. composed of learners from more than one language heritage, the learners themselves and their thoughts and experiences can be used as a resource. The teacher can actively engage the learners' identities in exchanging viewpoints about issues that enhance mutual understanding and socio-cultural support.

Monolingual classes are more complicated, as the teacher is forced to find other ways to promote learners' intercultural competence. One such way is to use 'critical incidents'. The teacher designs situations in which learners figuratively travel abroad, and are brought in direct contact with people from different countries and cultural backgrounds and presented with an incident that needs interpreting. It is a process that exposes them to cultural customs and surroundings different from their own and helps redefine their understanding of self and/or the surrounding world (Arthur, 2001). A similar method is organising immersion classes, where children are placed in educational settings where the target language is used. In such cases, learners study different subjects using the target foreign language. In this way, they become aware of the various learning strategies that they employ and pick up what they can without the direct involvement of a language tutor (Chamot and El-Dinary, 1999).

Teachers can and should also use technology to promote learners' intercultural competence. Critical incidents can be experienced via video-conferencing. O'Dowd (2000) reports the implementation of video-conferencing technology into a task-based environment in order to make learners more aware of how they view their own and the target cultures. Other studies report the use of the Internet for the promotion of intercultural education and anti-racism. The European Comenius project, EUROKID, involves secondary school teachers and students from three European countries in creating websites where groups from both minority and majority adolescent populations can exchange viewpoints about 'issues of acceptance, difference, racism, mixed cultures, (multiple) identities, and integration' (Gaine et al., 2003, p317).

Provided it is used with caution and monitored by trained tutors or parents, computer technology can enhance individual students' intercultural competence through foreign language learning. Whether at home or school (Tarozzi and Bertolini, 2000) or outside the strictly educational domain, as in ideas suggested by Linder, 2004, students can make use of the 'electronic learning networks' for enhancing intercultural learning (see Muller-Hartmann, 2000).

The case of English as an international/intercultural language

English has a significant role as an international/ intercultural language in the development of learners' intercultural identities. English is used by at least 670 million people with native or native-like fluency and, if the criterion of reasonable competence is used, then the grand total of speakers exceeds 1,800 million (Crystal, 1997, p61). It is also used in various intellectual, economic and cultural arenas around the world: Crystal (*ibid*) posits that it is employed by 85 per cent of the world's international organisations, 85 per cent of the world's motion pictures industry and 99 per cent of the pop music industry, whereas more than 80 per cent of the world's electronically stored information is in English. In Europe, English is used extensively as a *lingua franca* and is likely to play a key role in both the development and expression of European identity in the near future (Stalford, 2000). English is therefore a global language *par excellence* (McKay, 2002, p5), in the sense that it has acquired a 'special role that is recognised in every country' (Crystal, 1997, p2), either as an official language, or as a language that is given special priority as a foreign language.

This means that English is very likely to be the first, or only, foreign language that four out of five people on the planet will use for communication with speakers of other languages. In fact, this is the definition of the term 'international language' originally provided by Smith (1976), who identifies it as 'one which is used by people of different nations to communicate with one another' (p38). This makes English unique as a communicative tool between non-native communicators, since no other language has ever achieved this communicative status before in history.

English is also an important tool from a pedagogic point of view, as its educational history as a second or foreign language is long standing and special. Numerous projects have been developed to research different aspects of learning (for an extensive overview, see Ellis, 1997) and more are currently being developed that can help our understanding of the use of English as the international and intercultural language.

However, the use of English as a global language is not without negative effects. These effects are predominantly identified with the imperialistic history of English and its linguistic (Phillipson, 1992), socio-cultural (Pennycook, 1998) and even pedagogic (Canagarajah, 1999) implications (for a review of these issues, see Sifakis and Sougari, 2003). English is the conscious choice of whole nations who have decided to use it either as a key to their economic survival (as in Singapore – see Chew, 1999) or as a means of disseminating all sorts of cultural and religious information (the example of the use of 'English as an Asian language' in, for example, the Philippines, as discussed in Lourdes and Bautista, 1997).

English has certain indubitable advantages over other languages as the world's primary *lingua franca*. It is relatively easy to learn, with an uncomplicated grammar which can accommodate the use of a very extensive and ever-expanding vocabulary (Crystal, 1997). Furthermore, it bypasses the native/non-native divide (Kachru, 1985), which means that virtually all reasonably competent users of English can claim to 'own' the language in a way unprecedented for any other previous *lingua franca* (Higgins, 2003; Sifakis, 2004). This means that speakers who use English to communicate with people who speak other languages have only to be intelligible, in terms of clarity of pronunciation and basic lexical and semantic divergences (Schnitzer, 1995, p231). There are currently some interesting proposals being made for teaching intelligible world English (for example, Jenkins, 2000).

At the level of interculturality, and once the issue of intelligibility and comprehensibility is overcome, English is a unique tool for initial communication with people from other countries (Fox, 1997).

This is bound to facilitate the cultural, intellectual and emotional journey that is needed for the acquisition of intercultural competencies as well as for personal growth, especially for children. In this way, international English can serve the core values of interculturality, which are democracy, equality and participation, respect for cultural and linguistic plurality, internationalisation and ethnic diversity.

Implications for teachers

As Shi-Xu (2001, p279) writes:

> we teachers, trainers and consultants should try to introduce the discourses of diversity, equality, common goals and above all rational-moral motivation with respect to the Other-to society at large, starting with its youngest members possible. Methodologically, this work requires that we abandon the traditional role of imparting linguistic, cultural, and translation knowledge and try instead to develop a dialogue with students and practitioners through which we jointly initiate, (re-)formulate, debate and execute such new discourses.

Essentially, promoting intercultural competence means increasing learners' familiarity with foreign cultures, with one's own culture and with relationships between cultures. It also means acquiring the competence to learn cultures autonomously, following a student-centred autonomous learning approach. To this end, foreign language teachers and pedagogues should keep an open mind, avoid stereotyping, and do their best to expose learners to other cultures and viewpoints by encouraging the capacity to make critical decisions. Promoting intercultural competence by focusing on foreign language pedagogy also means young learners must be made aware of their own language rights (Skutnabb-Kangas, 2000) and prepared for global citizenship in a critical and reflective way.

> Rifts and violence only come about when discussion is no longer possible. Defending linguistic diversity and promoting the languages of minority communities therefore means giving peace another chance. 'You cannot be at peace with yourself or with others if you are forbidden to express yourself in the terms of your own

culture." A language conflict can degenerate into a cultural conflict and even into armed conflict. This issue is more than topical: the decision taken by authorities in Algeria to make Arabic the only official language provoked vivid reactions, especially in the Berber region, where the culture and the language have a strong hold. (L'Homme, 1998, p12)

As Sercu (2002, p72) says, language educators should realise that speaking a foreign language always means entering a cultural world that may to a lesser or a greater extent be different from one's own – 'therefore, all language education should always also be intercultural education'.

8

The development of early childhood education in Iceland: From women's alliance to National curriculum

Kristín Dýrfjörd

This chapter has two parts; the first gives the reader a glimpse of the Icelandic pre-school system and an overview of the history and current status of the Icelandic pre-school and the Icelandic family. The second part presents an outline of the national curriculum for pre-schools. The author was a member of a committee of four people who wrote the current national curriculum for the Ministry of Education.

Historical background of the Icelandic pre-school

The development of pre-school education or the daycare system in the western world can be divided into three main phases. First, day care for poor families, where children's basic needs for nutrition and emotional support were met. Second, kindergarten or half-day programmes that supplemented the family and gave children the opportunity to develop under the care of educated pre-school teachers. Third were laboratory schools that were mostly linked to universities (White and Buka, 1987). All pre-school education in Iceland followed the same principles. Pre-school traditions in Iceland can be traced back to 1924, when most of the inhabitants lived in rural areas of the country. In that year the Women's Alliance movement established an organisation that built and supervised the country's first pre-school. The organisation was named *Sumargjöf* (gift of summer), after an old Icelandic tradition related to the national holiday that is particularly connected with children. Even though the foundation of *Sumargjöf* was based on ideas from women, the first head of the organisation was a male teacher who studied at Columbia University in New York under Professor Kilpatrick, a follower of John Dewey. The first *Sumargjöf* pre-school was based and built on a blueprint from the Macmillan sisters' school in London. It was for children from poor families living under harsh conditions (Guomundsson, 1949). Until the 1940s pre-schools were mostly built for children of single parents and students, but then the original dream of the people in *Sumargjöf* came true: the first pre-school based on Fröebel's kindergarten principles was opened. This school was for children from middle-class families, where the mother usually was a house-wife working at home. It was decided that the kindergarten should be called a 'playschool', but the pre-school for socially underprivileged children was called a 'day care home' or a 'children's home'. In the first legislation on educational institutions for pre-school teachers there was a clause about 'laboratory schools', which never came into effect (Iceland, 1973).

The first trained pre-school teachers in Iceland sought their profes-sional education from the Nordic countries. At this time the Nordic pre-school movement was strongly influenced by Fröebel (Greve, 1994). At the same time, the leader and chair of *Sumargjöf* was influenced by the progressive movement. When the Pre-school Teachers' College was established by *Sumargjöf*, Valborg Sigurdar-dottir, a young woman educated in the United States, was elected leader. She was educated in the spirit of the new psychology of Gestalt, Piaget and the educational philosophy of Dewey. This back-ground suggests that the roots of Icelandic pre-schools were partly in Fröebel's kindergarten and his pedagogy built on the ideas of Rousseau and Pestalozzi, but were partly influenced by what was happening in the English-speaking world, based on the work of Kilpatrick and Dewey, and Piaget (Dýrfjörd, 2001b). Pre-school teachers today are educated in two universities in Iceland, The National Teacher University and University of Akureyri Educational

Department, both of which offer a three year BEd degree. At Akureyri there is an emphasis on creativity and philosophy in early childhood education.

For the next few decades pre-schools were mostly built and run by women's associations and/or by women's trade unions. By about 1970, when the second wave of the women's rights movement hit the western world, there was a strong movement in Iceland for the government to legislate to enable municipalities to build pre-schools and for the government to fund this.

Iceland's first Act for Pre-school Education dates from 1976 (Iceland, 1976). It obliged the State to finance part of the pre-school building costs, and defined pre-schools as educational institutions, falling under the responsibility of the Ministry of Education. Because pre-schools were seen as part of the educational establishment, by 1984 Iceland had its first draft of a National Curriculum for the Pre-school system, and in 1985 this was published as a formal National Curriculum. The term 'play-school' has been used in Iceland since 1991 (Iceland, 1991) to cover all kinds of pre-schools, nursery schools and early childhood centres. In 1994 the Pre-school system was the subject of another Act, which was the second in a few years. This set out, for the first time, that the government looked upon the Pre-school as the first stage of the country's formal educational system (Iceland, 1994, 1995b). In 1999 a new National Curriculum was published (Iceland, 1999a, 1999b). Although this was based on older versions, it was also completely different in that it was based on children's rights within the pre-school and was written with the child's point of view at its heart (Dýrfjörd, 2001a).

The 1994 Act sets out that every child has the right to attend a pre-school, and that the municipalities must make pre-school provision for all children. In theory, it is the parents' choice as to when children start pre-school. But although the law is clear, the municipalities have not been able to provide pre-school places for all children. Most pre-schools in Iceland are especially designed and purpose-built. Normally, a school has three or four classrooms and caters for 75 to 100 children. Building a new school is expensive and, following the 1991 Act, the state no longer participates in funding the construction, which is now the sole responsibility of each municipality.

Because the municipalities have not been able to provide pre-school places for all children, care for the youngest children outside the home still partly relies on daycare parents. In Reykjavík, the capital of Iceland and the largest city, the municipality has recently decided to offer free pre-school education for all five to six year-old children for three hours a day (Leikskólar Reykjavíkur, 2004). This acknowledges the importance of early formal education for children and the role of pre-schools.

In Iceland, between 93 and 94 per cent of all children aged three to six attend pre-schools, as do the majority of younger children after maternity leave has finished. Of all pre-school children, 72 per cent attend pre-school for more that seven hours a day, and 79 per cent of all children aged between one and six attend pre-school for part of the day (Hagstofan, 2004).

Two of the biggest threats to the pre-school system have been low wages and the high proportion of unskilled people in the workforce, who are most likely to change jobs. Trained teachers (with a BEd or other university degree) comprise just under 40 per cent of the workforce, the rest being less qualified. The child-adult ratio ranges from four to one for the youngest children up to ten to one for the oldest children (Regulation 225/1995). Those who work with children with special needs are not included in this ratio: 6.5 per cent of all children attending pre-school receive some kind of special education (Hagstofan, 2004). Inclusion is mandatory under the National Curriculum (Iceland, 1999b), so all children share pre-school and school classrooms. Some pre-schools may specialise in working with children with particular disabilities, but these children are always included with their peer group.

The Icelandic Family

The word 'family' suggests a particular image: this will generally be a picture of mother, father and children. In plural societies this picture is not the only one possible, and probably not even the most common. Most societies need broad and complex definitions to describe the family. In this chapter, the family is used to mean one or more adults who are responsible for the upbringing and welfare of one or more children, and create a home setting for this purpose. Ideas relating to many different possible images of the family are agreed upon: the nuclear family, as outlined above as a mother, father and children related through a bloodline, is a relatively new social concept and is fighting to survive today. Giddens (1982) believes that the nuclear family is a myth that appeared first in the nineteenth and twentieth centuries. However, it is clear that changing the concept of the family, both from within the family itself and from the society outside, affects children in various ways. It is therefore important to examine the frame that our society creates for the family. This includes looking at the working hours of parents. Working hours affect the family's ability to collaborate with their children's schools. It is not enough to give parents legal rights to collaborate with schools, or through public policy, if these parents do not have the opportunity to exercise their rights because of their working hours. If the adults in the family have to work long hours in order to provide basic needs, then the right the family is given, through law or regulation, is not realistic. Both the parents and the Pre-school must have the time to communicate and to work together. Throughout Icelandic history, until recent times, children's lives have been harsh. They had a heavy workload and their mortality rate was high (Gunnlaugsson, 1997). It was even believed, perhaps as a result of this mortality rate, that children were better off in Paradise. Throughout the history of our country it has been common for children to be born outside marriage. The explanation for this is partly that it was difficult for people to get married; couples had to own land and not owe money to society in order to be able to wed (Gunnlaugsson and Garoarsdóttir, 1997). This was the kind of society from which our families and our pre-schools have evolved.

Icelandic families: some facts
The population of Iceland in 2002 was 286,575. In the same year there were 4,091 live births, of which 41 per cent were first-born. The mean age for women to have children is 25 and 72 per cent of

these first born children were born to mothers between 20 and 29 years of age. The fertility rate is one of the highest in Western Europe, with just under 2.0 children per woman (Hagstofan, 2003).

Of newly born children, about 15 per cent are born to single parents, the remainder being born to married or cohabiting parents. In families with children, consensual unions comprise 27 per cent of two-parent families. Roughly 26 per cent of children in Iceland are living with one parent (Hagstofan, 2003).

Women form a large part of the Icelandic workforce, and just over 88 per cent of women between the ages of 24 and 54 work outside their home, with mean working hours of 34.5 hours a week. Men in the same age group work for 46.6 hours a week and about 97 per cent of them participate in the workforce (Hagstofan, 2003).

There is financial support for families with young children in Iceland through the tax system. Both parents are entitled to maternity leave for three months and another three months leave is also available, which parents can divide between them: the total family leave is nine months. The parents get an allowance, which covers the major part of income lost during this leave (Iceland, 1995b). It is common practice for one of the parents to stay at home with the child for over a year and also get part of their salary.

A large part of the early childhood educational system is financed and managed by the municipality. The few schools that are privately owned are also partly financed by the municipality: around 10 per cent of all pre-schools are privately owned. In 2003 there were 267 pre-schools, catering for 16,700 children (Hagstofan, 2004). Parents pay for the pre-school service on a sliding scale, according to their income/status. Parental contributions meet some 20 per cent to 50 per cent of the cost of running the schools (Dýrfjörd, 2001c; Hjartardóttir, 2001). The offer of partly free pre-schools in Reykjavík is therefore seen as an important contribution to the income of the families there.

Women are both a large and essential part of our labour market. Long working hours, coupled in many cases with running the household, affects how much time and energy mothers have to work in partnership with schools: the same is true for men. Long working hours are a part of the frame within which families live, and the school system must respect this. This working environment is a fact: the pre-school has to do what it can within this situation.

It is becoming more common for parents in Iceland who are divorced to share custody of the children. For example, of the 701 children whose parents divorced in 2001, the mother was given custody in just over 48 per cent of the cases, the father in 3.5 per cent of the cases, but shared custody was agreed upon in around 48 per cent of the cases (Hagstofan, 2003). It is clear that the State assumes that the child has a right to care from both parents. The relevant Act (Iceland, 1992) states that the parent who does not have custody has the right for information from the other parent and from the school about their child's well-being. This places a new and sometimes heavy burden on pre-school teachers, and makes the partnership between parents and school more complicated.

The Icelandic nation is, like the world at large, becoming more diverse. Till very recently, Icelandic society was homogenous. Today 6.6 per cent of the population were born in another country; this has risen from 3.9 per cent over just a few years. There were 5,844 children in Reykjavik pre-schools in 2001 (Hagstofan, 2003), and of these, 417 (about 7 per cent) spoke a language other than Icelandic. These children between them spoke 51 different languages, and were from 99 different nations (Leikskólar Reykjavíkur, 2003).

The pre-school community must be aware of the growing diversity of families and be willing and able to work with a wide range of people.

The national curriculum for the pre-school

The national curriculum for pre-schools will now be described and the main chapters outlined. The national curriculum makes it clear what rights children have, but does not set out how each school should accomplish these goals: that has to be each school's decision.

In Iceland a variety of pedagogical methods are used: the Waldorf pedagogy, the Reggio Emilia approach, and pedagogy based on American approaches such as the Bank Street curriculum, Kamii and de Vries methods and High Scope. Heuristic Play has also been gaining attention in recent years. There is also a method that has been developed in Iceland over the past decade, called the *Hjalli* method, which is based on gender segregation, minimal exposure to toys and artificial materials, external discipline and a highly organised daily schedule.

Most pre-schools adopt a variety of different approaches, to fit within the framework of the national curriculum. The openness of this frame lays an enormous responsibility on the pre-school teacher to act professionally. One of the problems for pre-schools is the high turnover of poorly-trained staff, and the scarcity of trained pre-school teachers. The national curriculum presents challenges, but is also very rewarding.

The national curriculum is divided into eight chapters, and is 47 pages long. Each chapter addresses a particular concept.

The pre-school
The first chapter sets out the goals for the pre-school and how they should be achieved. Pre-schools are expected to empathise with children's play and creativity, and should not aim to instruct children in specific areas of knowledge. The aim is to develop the child's maturity, not to impart specific subject matter but to address physical and motor development, emotional, cognitive and language development, social development and consciousness, aesthetic development and creativity, and ethical development and morality.

Play and pre-school activities
Chapter two concerns the daily life of children in the pre-school: the importance of play is particularly emphasised. The relationship between play and creativity is explored, and the importance of the environment is emphasised as the 'third teacher' in the pre-school, after peers and teachers. The influence from the Reggio Emila philosophy is clear here. The teachers' role in play is examined, as well as

the importance of the peer group. Teachers are encouraged to use pedagogical documentation as a tool to understand children's learning, as well as to develop themselves professionally. Inclusion is mandated, mainly through discussion on the special needs of children and how the pre-school must meet every child at his or her own standpoint. A particular section is dedicated to life-skills and their importance for children. These life skills include being brought up to be an active member of a democratic society. To accomplish this it is required that children should be active participants in planning the curriculum, and should join in the evaluation of the pre-school. This comes from the view that the child is an able and competent player in her/his own life. The function of rules that correspond to the maturity of the child are especially examined. Finally, the importance of a daily rhythm and schedule in the school is given attention.

The pre-school learning areas

In chapter three the pre-school learning areas are defined, and special attention is given to the rights of the child within certain areas. The learning areas include motor development, language development, creativity, music, nature and environment, culture and society. These learning areas should overlap and be integrated into everyday basic pre-school activities.

In the section on motor development special attention is given to outdoor play, which has played an important part in Icelandic society's ideas about child rearing. In the pre-school where the timetable has become crowded, the idea of having long periods of time outside in free activity is appealing.

Language development is an important area. This includes conversation, both that which comes freely, but also organised conversation, as is applied in philosophy for children (Lipman, 1991). Iceland has a cultural heritage full of sagas and oral stories. This heritage is reflected in the emphasis placed on literature and language development, as well as emergent reading, writing and mathematical skills. Children should be exposed to a variety of ways of expressing themselves artistically, and art and music are expected to be a large part of every child's pre-school education.

The national curriculum states that humanity is dependent for its existence upon nature and natural forces. Knowledge of nature and of natural phenomena is thus of vital importance, especially in a country like Iceland where the weather can be dangerous and nature harsh. Children need to become acquainted with the great variety in nature, to come into direct contact with it and to learn to enjoy it. A child's mind needs to be opened to the beauty of nature and she/he should learn to respect and develop responsibility towards the natural world. Finally, it emphasises that the child's experience of nature should be an integral part of play and artistic creation. This emphasis on the natural world and the role of nature and the weather is rooted in Iceland's history.

Awareness of cultural diversity is important and should be given room in the curriculum. Children first learn about their own close cultural environment but also to respect and value other peoples' backgrounds and traditions. Understanding and respect are key-words.

Partnership between home and school
The fourth chapter is about the partnership between home and school. It is clearly set out that parents bear the primary respon-sibility for the life and education of their children, but that the pre-school must support parents in their role and give them help. A close relationship between home and school is recommended, and it is pointed out that it parents know their children best. They have fol-lowed the child's development from birth and possess unique know-ledge of the child. The relationship between home and school begins before the child goes to school, starting when the parents first get notice of acceptance into the school. In Iceland most children attend pre-school close to their homes, in accordance with most muni-cipality policies. It is therefore likely that parents know both the school's reputation and other families who attend the same school. The national curriculum asks head teachers to give parents general information about the school, the curriculum and how their child's

first days are going to be organised. The head teacher must outline the national curriculum to the parents. Most children start pre-school at around two years of age (89 per cent, Hagstofan, 2004) and settling in takes about four to six days, depending on children and parents. During this time parents are expected to stay with their children in the pre-school, all day at first, but decreasing to just a few minutes on the last day. For some children a longer settling in time is needed. Because this process of adaptation is fairly well known, most parents and employers know that this may happen. The national curriculum points out that it is important to use the settling in time to build up trust and knowledge between the school and parents: during this period the foundation is laid for the partnership between home and school.

The parent's rights and duties to share information with the school is emphasised in the national curriculum: parents have rights to ask for meetings and to be able to contact staff.

Connection between pre-school and compulsory school

In chapter five the connections between pre-school and compulsory school is outlined. Both cooperation and formal connection are necessary, and head teachers from both schools are made jointly responsible.

The school curriculum

Chapter six is about the school curriculum which each school has to construct. This is a policy statement on pedagogy, and an overview of the daily routine and activities in the school. Each school must recognise the cultural and social environment of its community. The national curriculum sets out that the school curriculum must be written and be accessible. Each school has to involve parents in constructing the school curriculum. The importance of all staff participating in preparing and discussing what goes into the school curriculum is stressed. A full discussion of the different approaches and underlying pedagogical philosophies should take place, which becomes a platform on which the pedagogical work of the school is based.

The school evaluation

School evaluation is the subject of chapter seven of the national curriculum documents; both self-evaluation and external evaluation. Self-evaluation should be the foundation for professional development in the school as well as an essential part of the school curriculum. All staff, children and parents are expected to participate in this process. Evaluations always conclude with a written report, which sets out how the data was collected, who the stakeholders were, the main findings, weakness and strengths. Finally, it must be shown how the findings will be used to improve the school. Every year the Ministry of Education chooses two pre-schools at random for external evaluation.

Formal school development projects

It chapter eight the Ministry of Education sets out how it will promote school development projects. The Ministry has grants which schools can apply for, and the procedure for grant application is explained.

Conclusion

The history of pre-school education in Iceland is not extensive, compared to other Nordic countries, but is rich and productive. It has moved away from the idea that pre-school is for children in underprivileged situations to pre-schools being seen as the right of every child. This right is independent of the parent's job or financial status, and is a right which is granted to all children. Most children start pre-school at around two years of age and stay there for up to nine hours a day. How the staff of the schools communicate what happens in the pre-school and how parents are given insight into the children's day is fundamental. Pedagogical documentation is appreciated both as a tool for professional development for the teachers but also and not least as an opportunity for parents to get to know more about what their children are doing during the day, and about how their intellectual skills are developing. This can be a much-needed bridge, and research into this part of the national curriculum would be most interesting. The pre-school community in Iceland is small and relatively few people are involved in research. The influence of the national curriculum from 1999 has not been formally examined. But it is common knowledge that requiring each school to write its own curriculum has made schools take a stand and outline their work. The same is true for self-evaluation. Reykjavík, where around a third of all pre-schools in the country are located, has decided to offer three hours a day of free pre-school education for all five to six year-old children. This followed detailed discussions with business enterprise representatives, who felt that Iceland had to get an educational edge. One way to get this edge would be to start compulsory schooling earlier. But after examining this matter, the capital's decision was to offer this free pre-school provision, and the Minister of Education has endorsed this in the media. There currently seems to be an alignment between the pre-school society and the politicians – but the gatekeepers of the pre-school must stay alert.

III: Teaching and Learning

9

Children's perspectives on citizenship education in primary education textbooks

Luisa de Freitas

This chapter begins by briefly summarising key aspects of textbook research, focusing particularly on Portugal. Studies of the values implicit in primary education texts deserve greater attention. Textbooks in Portugal follow national guidelines, so it is possible to describe how citizenship education is included in these guidelines since 1986. The chapter then discusses the findings of a study which replicates an earlier analysis of children's views of the textbooks they use and of the values portrayed in them.

Research on textbooks

Research on school texts has been developed in several countries using a variety of approaches (Chopin, 1992; CIDREE, 1994; Castro *et al.*, 1999; Elliot and Woodward, 1990). Anyon points out that 'textbooks are social products that can be examined in the context of their time, place and function' (1979, p361). The importance attached to research studies into textbooks and their focus varies from country to country and from one subject to another. Stray considers that textbooks were only taken as a serious object of study in the 1980s, when 'they moved firmly on the scholarly agenda' (1994, p1). Elliot and Woodward (1990) consider that the most significant change in textbooks in recent decades followed research on school reforms and on teaching, and of strong criticism of textbooks.

Wade, reviewing ten years of content analysis of social studies texts in *Theory and Research on Social Studies* (1993), suggests that not only textbooks deserve criticism, but also the research undertaken on them. She identifies five topics for research: themes (such as propaganda), groups (specific groups, cultures, countries), historical events, comprehension (related to literary studies) and disciplinary or inter-disciplinary approaches. She finds that the purpose of most studies was to describe the characteristics of a particular topic, to draw inferences about the findings, and to infer what effect the text might have on students. The latter type of study is particularly valued by Wade, who considers that, although this research was not published in social studies journals, it had a strong impact on the social studies community. She advocates that multi-disciplinary research teams should 'go beyond simply analysing the content of social studies texts and undertake more studies in the classroom focused on understanding the effects that textbook learning has on students' (1993, p249). This approach influenced the initial textbook research by the author of this chapter. However, this was not the main focus of other textbook research in Portugal, which was closer to the approach identified by Shen (1994), who pointed to the increase in studies that focused on race, ethnicity, gender, and social values and ideology since the 1970s, and specifically relates these issues to the textbook industry and to the role textbooks play in social and cultural reproduction.

Research on textbooks in Portugal
Research on textbooks in Portugal was one of the first research fields to have public relevance, and it has continued to be one of the most important research themes. Several studies were completed in the 1970s, the most remarkable being *Ensino Primário e Ideologia* (Primary Education and Ideology) by Maria de Fátima Bivar (1971). Many other studies followed, analysing Portuguese language textbooks for primary schools with objectives that were based on this pioneer study:

> Textbooks can be considered cultural texts, representing a particular cultural environment, bearing within them values and specific

images which we should consider ... We need to find out what kind of cultural patterns they convey, what kind of dynamic and family structure they offer, how much they value work and play, what images they mediate from infancy, which experiences of the natural environment they underline, the place of national identity in how we are included in society ... what kind of ethical proposals and models of behaviour textbooks present (Bivar, 1971, pp21-22).

The analyses of primary school textbooks made during the 1970s were the most significant. Examples of academic research include the documentation of arguments (Mónica, 1978); examining gender issues (Brandão, 1979; Leal, 1979); and analysing the presentation of historical events (Radich, 1979). As Bivar points out, all of these could be categorised as the analysis of values and models of behaviour.

This kind of analysis, sometimes integrated within very personal and focused studies, continues to be the most common and interesting of the varied researchers in the area, who come from several social sciences, literature, history, sociology and anthropology, as well as from education (Almeida, 1991; Barca and Fonte, 1989; Barreno, 1982; Cortesão, 1982; Fernandes, 1987; Martins, 1992; Matos, 1990; Simões, 1987).

The first study of textbooks for basic education in schools was a joint project of the Ministry of Education and the University of Lisbon Education Department in the Faculty of Sciences. Textbooks were analysed by subject area specialists, following a common framework that included a socio-cultural and ideological perspectives, as well as a scientific/pedagogic perspective. The study included analysis of the three textbook functions identified by Chopin (1992). Apple (1986) suggests that a defining characteristic of textbooks is their powerful influence on what is taught and learned in schools. As Valente, the project coordinator, stressed, 'the study intended to show how the authors of a textbook, starting from an analysis of the official curriculum, interpreted these objectives, presenting proposals diminishing or improving the aims' (1989, p12).

In primary school environmental studies textbooks the main focus was scientific, but there are also several references to values. Basic values were included in most books, whilst the importance of co-operation and participation in group work seldom appeared, values related to critical thinking, freedom, creativity, responsibility, religion and national identity were never included, and many examples of gender stereotypes and bias were evident.

It is not possible to present a complete overview of textbook research in the 1990s. Several studies were presented in teachers' association conferences and publications, and many were part of postgraduate projects, mainly as part of in-service courses. The Proceedings of the International Meeting on Textbooks (Castro, Rodrigues, Silva and Sousa, 1999) gives a reasonable overview of the situation in Portugal, including reference to the only two studies listening to students' voices: the author's study in primary schools (Freitas, 1999) and Bento's study (1999) of secondary students.

An international study of texts for older students also included studies of students' opinions (Pais, 1999). The well-known IEA study on civic education did not include primary education textbooks. However, these texts may be crucial for citizenship education: it has been suggested that the use of textbooks could contribute 'to maintain the preservation of Portuguese self-image as tolerant people without trying to confront the challenge our real stereotypes and preconceptions' (Menezes, Xavier and Cibele, 1997, p45).

Marques (1997) reports on a study of environmental studies textbooks, suggesting that, whilst all official documents attribute similar importance to values, textbooks in practice diminish their significance. A more recent study by the *Comissão para a Igualdade e para os Direitos das Mulheres* [Equality and Rights for Woman Commission] focuses on gender representation in primary school textbooks in Portuguese language and mathematics, and showed a persistent emphasis on gender stereotypes and bias, and few gender-free values (Correia and Ramos, 2002). Another study (Santos, 2001) of natural sciences texts focused on citizenship education, and found that scientific aspects were dominant, even where there were good opportunities for citizenship values and approaches to be used. This study is rigorous and deep, and concludes that natural science textbooks could contribute significantly to citizenship education, but that the textbooks analysed did not provide education for active citizenship because 'the interaction between the cognitive dimension and the formative dimension of science education is very weak' (p252).

Citizenship education in Portuguese official documents

The Comprehensive Law on the Education System (Portugal, 1986) translates the citizenship principles of the Portuguese Republic Constitution into formal educational provision. It stresses that the education system:

- contributes to the full and balanced development of individual personalities, encouraging the education of free, responsible, autonomous and supportive citizens' (article 2, §4)

- [and] ... develop democratic and pluralistic ideals which embody respect for others and their ideas and is open to dialogue and free exchange of opinions, forming citizens able to constructively criticise their social system and capable of working towards its progressive transformation (article 2, §5)

- [The system should be organised to ensure civic and moral education of young people (article 3, c)

- [and] ensure the right to be different with respect for individual personalities and ambitions and consideration and appreciation of different learning and cultures (article 3, d)

The objectives of basic education also set out several statements on citizenship education

- to develop national awareness open to realities in a context of universalistic humanism and international solidarity and co-operation (article 7, f)

- to further the acquisition of independent attitudes so as to develop citizens who have civic responsible and participate democratically in community life (article 7, i)

119

Ways of operating and implementing these statements have been discussed and tried over the past two decades. The concept of personal and social development was prevalent during the educational reform movement in the late 1980s and early 1990s. Between 1996 and 2001 the essential competencies for basic education were the subject of a wide-ranging debate, that included how to integrate citizenship education, either as a set of specific courses (a subject) or as a transversal curriculum dimension which is integrated into all subjects. By the end of the twentieth century official documents began to use the term citizenship education, comprising civic education, personal and social development and moral education.

In the midst of these discussions, a revised version of the Curriculum Organisation and Syllabi (*Organização Curricular e Programas*) for the first stage of basic education was produced (Ministério da Educação, 1998). Originally published in 1991, this new edition introduced some significant alterations explaining the general objectives for the first stage of basic education: these were now categorised in three dimensions or broad general objectives:

• personal dimension of education

• essential basic and intellectual acquisitions

• citizenship dimension

Specific objectives for each dimension were defined, including seven specific objectives for citizenship. Some of these simply rephrase or repeat ideas and principles described above, but some elements – such as consumer education – are introduced for the first time. This new edition of *Curriculum Organisation and Syllabi* is the one document that every primary teacher should know well and follow as the syllabus for primary education.

A new curriculum organisation for basic education was established by Decree-Law 6/2001 (Portugal, 2001). An innovative feature of this curriculum was the establishment of cross-curricular dimensions (*formações*) and non-subject-specific areas set alongside traditional subjects or disciplinary areas. Citizenship education is defined as one of three cross-curricular dimensions, an important transversal dimension covering the whole curriculum. A curriculum 'guiding principle' in article 3 d) specifies the 'integration of citizenship education, as a cross curricular feature, in all areas'.

To make the orientation of this Decree-Law even more explicit, the General Directorate of Basic Education published an extensive document entitled *National Curriculum for Basic Education: Essential Competencies* [Currículo Nacional do Ensino Básico – Competências Essenciais] (Ministério da Educação, 2001), based on broad public discussion and on the experience of implementing the new guidelines in a group of schools over several years.

This document is not easy to analyse. The idea of citizenship education is not very accurately transferred from the Decree-Law 6/2001 into the National Curriculum document in the introduction or in the sections which are common to all subjects. For example the terms 'citizenship' or 'citizenship education' are not used: only the term 'civic education' is employed.

Ten general 'key competencies' for basic education stressed the principles and values of the Comprehensive Law on the curriculum. The general citizenship education principles of the Decree-Law are:

- the development and awareness of personal and social identity

- participation in civic life freely, responsibly, critically and with solidarity

- respect and value for individual and group differences relating to behaviour and choices

- development of ecological awareness to promote, value and preserve the natural and cultural heritage

- value for the relational dimensions of learning and for ethical relationships between knowledge and people.

Most of the ten *Essential Competencies* relate in some way to citizenship education, but three of them are crucial to citizenship education:

- adopting appropriate problem-solving strategies and decision-making strategies

- carrying out activities independently, responsibly and creatively

- cooperating with others in common tasks and projects

These competencies are largely discussed in the document in the context of traditional subjects, and *Essential Competencies* includes 'specific essential competencies' for each subject in the National Curriculum, which are derived from the General Essential Competencies. It also includes suggestions for learning experiences to develop these general competencies over the period of children's compulsory education.

An analysis of how these 'Specific Essential Competencies' could integrate citizenship education shows that the contribution of subjects is not very significant. The Specific Essential Competencies focus on competencies that directly include, or could be related to, the cognitive dimensions of specific subject- information, knowledge and the processes to construct this. It is assumed that the national curriculum 'is geared to the use of teaching methods that encourage active learning (learning by doing and experimental learning) but this principle accommodates a variety of approaches' (EURYDICE, 2002, p106).

A framework was constructed to analyse the textbooks and students' answers based on references to citizenship education, and in particular the specific objectives in *Curriculum Organisation and Syllabi – first cycle of basic education* (Ministério da Educação, 1998).

Citizenship education in a 1998 research study

In 1998 I carried out a broad study of environmental studies, both physical and social textbooks, with the aim of understanding both teachers' and parents' points of view, and children's perspectives. Our conceptions of childhood changed in the 1990s: the way we listened to children changed. Developments in the field of sociology (such as Chrisholm, Büchner, Krüger and Bois-Reymond, 1995; Postman, 1995) show researchers trying to understand children's

122

culture and opinions, on the assumption that 'even small children are as credible and important to listen to as are adults' (Näsman, von Gerber and Hollmer, 1999, p231). *The Convention on the Rights of the Child*, adopted by the United Nations General Assembly on 20 November 1989, and in particular the twelfth and thirteenth articles, could not be ignored in these new approaches to study children's lives.

The part of this study that focused on children's perspectives included the views of 144 primary pupils from nine classes in the first to fourth grade of basic elementary education. They were drawn from the classes of teachers who were cooperating with the University of Minho in primary teachers education during 1997-98. The objective was to understand how children used and understood their environmental studies textbooks:

- What kind of textbooks would they like to have?

- What did they like and dislike most in their textbooks, and why?

- What aspects did they find easier or more difficult in their textbooks, and why?

It was anticipated that children's preferences, likes and dislikes would be mainly related to the different topics, and be centred on illustrations or suggested activities. I also expected that a significant set of answers would show concern for the environment. I did not have specific or preconceived expectations about how they perceived their identity, whether personal, social or national.

The students answered two open-ended questions about a short story which was read to them about their preferences for the following year's environmental textbooks. Content analyses showed that teacher influence was evident in some classrooms, but not in most. Answers were grouped into three main categories: subject matter (163), illustration (116), and quizzes (15). Many answers (200) fell into the further category of values.

Children were also asked to identify three pages of the textbook which they particularly liked or disliked, and two pages they felt to be easy or difficult, and they were asked to give reasons for this. They enjoyed this activity, and it appears that teachers gave them total freedom to respond to this task. The full results of this large-scale survey are not relevant to this chapter, but they confirmed that the responses to the open questions and to values were even more significant. Within the category of values, fewer responses occurred in the sub-category of environmental issues (for example, preventing pollution) than expected, and many more responses in the sub-category of local and national identity. Marques (1997) stressed that basic values related to health care, hygiene, and safety and national identity values were the most common in the textbooks he analysed. Other answers related to showing respect for others. Children 'saw' much more in the texts than the authors intended, either explicitly or implicitly. For example, one child selected a page on the topic of communications that showed several small pictures of a woman at work as one that she disliked: the choice was justified 'I don't like the secretary. She seems very arrogant to me'. Significant numbers of responses of this kind were related to explicitly or perceived behaviour. Most of these involved judgements of behaviour, such as showing, or not showing, respect and understanding for others.

Four main points arise from this part of the study:

- Students were sensitive about values education. They found more value-related content in the textbooks than the authors intended

- More attention was given to behaviour showing negative values than to that showing positive values

- Students did the task carefully and presented personal justifications. It was not easy to interpret their opinions

- Textbooks could be a powerful vehicle for citizenship education (Freitas, 2000, p255)

The 2004 study: how children view citizenship education in their textbooks

Citizenship education took on an increasingly important role in educational discussion in Portugal from the mid-1990s. Many books and articles encouraged teachers to be aware of the significance of citizenship education.

It was therefore decided to replicate the 1998 study in 2004, focusing particularly on the part of the study described above. Children were surveyed from the same schools as in the 1998 study, and the sample included 54 second year students from two classrooms in two different schools, 45 third year students from two classrooms in two schools and 69 fourth year students from three classrooms in two schools. A qualitative content analysis approach was again used, which was based on the ten categories in the framework of the policy document.

The development of systematic and critical thinking
Despite the very different approaches shown in the variety of textbooks, all of them provoked systematic and critical thinking by the children. The children's answers showed the level of this critical thinking: many fourth grade children strongly argued that the texts they looked at included too much about the history of Portugal, and also that this history was written in a way that was difficulty for them to understand. In their responses to the open-ended questions, many rejected this approach to history. Although the writer supports the introduction of history in primary school, and the national syllabus suggests studying everyday life in certain periods, this is not the kind of history in current textbooks, which present traditional political history in a chronological and fact-heavy manner.

Children's responses included comments such as: 'It is on fights and has many dates to memorise', and 'I do not like politics'. A response to the open-ended questions was 'I would hate to have an Environmental Studies textbook only about history and kings, since I hate history and I never will like it because it is very boring and stressful. I do not like history because I have to know the names of kings, and dates of important events that happened in Portugal'.

125

Although there were answers like these in all classrooms, more were found in one particular class. Other children commented that they liked history, and the history presented in their textbooks. One child wrote 'It is about things that are very important for me'. Opinions do not seem to have been influenced by teachers. Almost every fourth grade student referred to the 34 pages of history (in a text-book of 144 pages).

A similar mixture of contradictory opinions was given in response to the topic of cultural heritage found in the third grade textbook. Several students responded to the open-ended question by saying that they do not like studying cultural heritage because it is 'badly done', and the pictures used are 'not nice'. Others said they like the topic, without offering any explanation.

Portuguese language textbooks were found to be aiming to develop systematic and critical thinking, but this critical thinking was not evident in the mathematics textbooks.

The development of problem solving and decision making competencies: autonomy, creativity and responsibility
Textbooks attempt to develop competencies of autonomy, creativity and responsibility through a variety of activities related to inquiry and group work. However, some students appear not to like these very much. For example, one student designated a page as difficult 'because I have to suggest many things'.

Mathematics didactics assumes that one of its specific methodolo-gies is problem solving. The study analysed how problem solving was presented in mathematics textbooks. Although many problems are presented to be solved, these concern stereotyped situations that bear no relationship to social issues.

The development of autonomous work: competencies to act responsibly, alone and collectively, in community problems and tasks
Textbooks ask for written answers in response to questions, provid-ing space for replies. Many also ask for issues to be discussed with colleagues. They suggest groups and panels, and some include 'post-

it' materials to help organise and stimulate discussion. Some suggest interviews with members of communities and visits to institutions. One fourth year textbook suggests activities and interventions in the community. Most textbooks concentrate these activities towards the end of each topic, and children often felt that this was too much to do. This view was often connected with the next point.

The development of competencies for cooperation with others in common tasks (negotiating and respecting rules, assuming roles, assuming responsibilities and managing conflicts peacefully)
These textbooks tend to suggest that children in class engage in a great deal of group work. However, they do little to develop the competencies needed for effective group work, and children did not select these pages because there was no support provided for group work.

The development and awareness of personal and social identity (basic values, self knowledge and self-esteem, – relationships, and Portuguese /European/ Global identity)
There are specific topics on each aspect, and information texts cover all the suggested material in the syllabus. However, this may not be sufficient for individual students' level of development, though they could find more information from other sources. In many cases the information is unrelated to values, as this might be seen as indoctrination. Some textbooks include pictures, and students are asked to construct rules or processes to follow. One text gave a long list on what to do about issues to do with heath, hygiene and safety. Fourth grade students list fewer basic values than do second and third grade children, and use knowledge about themselves and their families. Another book included a picture showing drunken people: this page was frequently selected by children as being disliked. One boy explained why: 'I do not like bad animals that kill people. And a drunk should not be shown in books, in order to have a world without drunken people'. Another boy justified his selection of the same page: 'I want to prevent my parents from drinking too much alcohol'. This class, in a school located in a socially deprived neighbourhood, produced a number of examples of children wanting a more rose-tinted world.

In relation to Portuguese, European and Global identity, textbooks include a great deal of information about national identity, but this information might also be capable of development by some students in alternative ways. There is very little information relating to European identity, usually only a map; and for global identity there is often just a world map showing the distribution of the Portuguese language. Students either liked or disliked this, but were not neutral on the subject. It would be possible to have made more references to globalisation related to trade, for example. Overall, it appears that though some textbooks are giving greater emphasis to national identity, sometimes the reverse is true.

The development of ecological awareness, promoting, valuing and preserving natural and cultural heritage
Where textbooks cover this issue, there are very few references to consumer education. Students were less interested in ecological problems and the preservation of cultural heritage, though some classes gave it a lot of attention in the open-ended questions. One third grade class practically ignored the subject: the textbook they were using showed pollution relating to the use of cars rather than to factories. In one picture a boy was using a mask because of the polluted environment: only two children selected this page.

Respecting and valuing individual and group differences (cultural, ethnic, gender, social, age-related, and special needs)
There were explicit and implicit differences between textbooks on this subject: it was not generally given the attention that some official documents suggested it should have; nor do Essential Competencies include a competence specifically related to valuing diversity. Students give little attention to this subject. In the few cases in which these issues are raised in the textbooks, children say they do not like these pages.

The development of an awareness of the interrelationships among different socio-economic groups and a willingness to interact and participate responsibly and with solidarity

This could be understood as related to globalisation and been introduced in relation to trade. But texts did not draw attention to it: it seemed to be interpreted as differences between occupations and jobs. The topic on professions was not developed in depth, and there was nothing about poverty. Generally, a middle-class vision was dominant. Careful analysis of the case studies presented in a fourth year unit which contained problem-solving material, showed that they were not absolutely value-free, and were middle-class and gender biased. Women were never the principal characters in these situations. The oldest textbook in use in these classes was a 1992 Portuguese language textbook: this was the only textbook that included texts about poverty.

Participation in civic life – freely, responsibly, with solidarity and critically

Fourth grade textbooks proposed a few activities in this area, but students generally ignored them.

Valuing the relational dimensions of learning and the ethical relationship between knowledge and people

This item could be related to aspects of the item on identities and co-operative working, but few students refer to relationships when working with colleagues, apart from saying that they should not fight.

Conclusion

Although official documents contain much about citizenship education, they are abstract and general: more specific suggestions for teachers and for textbook authors are needed.

Children look carefully at their textbooks. They selected diverse items which show different points of view about almost everything. What they most agreed upon was their like or dislike for Portuguese history and cultural heritage: some found it easy, others difficult. They also were also explicit about their difficulties with community institutions, because they did not understand them. They were aware of basic values and competencies related to citizenship education. Negative representations about basic values and relationships interested students more than positive ones. Children did not pay significant attention to cultural differences.

There are many significant differences between environmental studies textbooks: it would be interesting to list the best features of each, and bring all of these together as the basis for a good book. While the books pay some attention to citizenship education, some do so poorly, and miss opportunities to include more information on certain topics. In most areas, the connection with citizenship education is missed: this was particularly evident in Portuguese language textbooks. While several texts include values, these were not adequately explored. Sometimes there are questions asking for children's opinions, but not consistently. Is it a teacher's function to explore children's opinions? Textbooks include suggestions for activities that are ignored by children, probably because they seem too difficult. The approaches to several social environment topics need to be reconsidered: children identify them as difficult, and did not understand them. Environmental studies textbooks could have been an effective, though controversial, way to approach basic values and citizenship values, but this did not happen. Citizenship education is a cross-curricular dimension that is invisible in mathematics textbooks. There were also considerable differences between the role given to citizenship education in Portuguese language and environmental studies textbooks. One first year environmental studies text is an example of a promising first step to promoting citizenship education, using a well-designed constructivist approach. This was the most careful approach: it seems that it should be possible to have a similar textbook for each of the other primary school years.

10

Art and citizenship: a joint venture or a fatal attraction?

Hugo Verkest

Visual literacy: a way to survive

One of the tests my seven year-old daughter had to undertake to determine the extent of her dyslexia involved a 'rapid naming test' that assessed her capacity to retain numbers and images. Given that dyslexia is inherited, presumably from me, I was intrigued to find that she had impressive skills of visual recall. Given sets of images, she could read and remember them and make interesting comparisons between them. Children with dyslexia have, more than other children, what can be described as a kind of mental database, which they access to carry out creative or analytical work. Some areas of visual culture are less available to young people, and they cannot understand art without a full range of visual references.

In November 2003 I was again surprised when I went with my daughter's class to visit the exhibition designed by Umberto Eco which focused on a single masterpiece by Titian, the *Venus of Urbino* (1538). Detective-like, Eco investigated different aspects of the content and the form of this painting (Eco, 2003). His conception identified three parts: the genesis of the painting and its influence from and on other painters; the iconography of Venus and, thirdly, an amazing analysis of a detailed web of artefacts, music and poems. The class ventured through time and space: in every room they met a kind of philosophical 'aha!' – *Erlebnis*. On each occasion, these twelve year-old girls and boys made fascinating observations. In the final room they were shown paintings by Picasso, Modiglianni, Delvaux and Dali, and recognised how these modern artists had been influenced by Titian: they spontaneously compared them with the original and interpreted details of the pieces of modern art.

When we returned to see the masterpiece from the Uffizi Gallery in Firenze, there was a strong silent moment when forty eyes looked very carefully at the painting, whispering their comments and expressing their impressions. They remembered much about the paintings. To me this was good example of the re-contextualisation of a mythological painting (Boeve, 1999). After walking through rooms featuring jewellery, dress and architecture, on themes such as nakedness, the social position of the wife, the influence of mythology on sixteenth century society, the painting was empowered with stories and personal impressions and given a new frame, full of links to the past, present and future. The modern artists recycled the older material and themes into their paintings.

In the evaluation which followed the visit, most of the children participated enthusiastically in the critical talk, not least those with dyslexia – probably because the input of visual elements inspired them more than any words in a textbook could have done.

This suggests that one of the most relevant ways to introduce citizenship might be through visual literacy, rather than using theoretical argumentation. One of the best visual literacies might be the use of cartoons, combined with critical and philosophical discussion, particularly for children with restricted abilities who might benefit more from well-chosen illustrations than from well-written stories. The experiences I have outlined confirmed to me that we should not ignore visual literacy when introducing children to citizenship.

Visual literacy: a way to initiate children into citizenship
Children have a certain level of either historical or contemporary 'visual literacy (Messaris, 1994). We need to help children become familiar with and understand a wide range of cultural practices around visual literacy with which we, as teachers, are already familiar, so that pupils can read a silent film and appreciate an exhibition.

Which skills might assist them to develop these complex artistic practices? We cannot put art in a vacuum, and a full range of visual references and expression is required. This is a matter of acquiring a deep understanding of the ways in which visual representation has been used in cultural traditions, so that they can be used in a sophisticated, flexible and inventive way. There are two kinds of visual literacy. One kind can be taught, through exposure and familiarity, and by connecting an object with the context of its creation. This kind of visual literacy pre-supposes the existence of a mental database which pupils and students can access to carry out the creative or analytical work they wish to do. The other kind is based on experiences of dyslexia. This visual literacy is a distinctive visual interest or interest in the ways things can be visually transmitted or represented. Children with special needs may have brains wired to grasp the world more clearly through visualisation and from visual information (Pollock, 1988, 2000).

This activation of visual literacy is supported by Paivio's *dual code* theory of memory (1986): he suggests that, if the aim is for information to sink in, the use of two memory tracks, verbal and non-verbal, to present subject material is far better than just one track. Illustrations influence the capacity to memorise texts in a positive way: cartoons also activate relevant foreknowledge. The increased use of illustrations in textbooks may result from the multifunctional use of methods such as recreational reading of instruction books, books meant to be read, and reference books. The picture plays an important mediating role in the processes of learning and decoding problems in this multi-form use of educational tools as a teacher-substitute.

Several functional supports for cognitive acquisition come from visual material: in the representative sense, the visual makes the text concrete; in the organisational sense, it helps gives order and coherence to the text; in the interpretative sense, it clarifies events and abstract concepts which may be difficult to understand; and in the transformative sense, it lightens the memory. Winn (1987) regards the strongly verbally-orientated school tradition as an obstacle when using diagrams to improve cognitive learning processes like visual clustering or mental imagination. Children with a strongly-developed right hemisphere, who are therefore more able to incorporate three-dimensional information, may benefit from this.

Educational practitioners have so far shown little interest in the critical production and interpretation of graphic communication, despite the enormous use of visual material in our society. Picture books were meant for unlettered pre-school children, and comics were considered to be inferior literature. It was thought that they make children lazy because reading played only a minor role: 'watching' was, by definition, a passive occupation.

The idea of a multi-tracked supply of information connects with Howard Gardner's (1983, 1993) reflections on the nature and development of intelligence, particularly of spatial intelligence. Children with strong spatial intelligence think in images and pictures: they may be fascinated with mazes or jigsaw puzzles, or spend their free time drawing, building with Lego or day-dreaming. Van der Leij (1994) points out that dyslexic people have insufficient opportunities to show their strong visual three-dimensional side.

The subversive role of cartoons

While caricatures originated around the Mediterranean, cartoons developed in a cooler climate. The Protestant Reformation in Germany made use of visual propaganda to underline the proclamations of Luther. An excellent example of Luther's use of visual protest is seen in two woodcuts from the pamphlet *Christ and Antichrist*, originally drawn by Lucas Cranach the Elder. These contrast the actions of Jesus with those of the church hierarchy. The two pictures are clearly intended to raise public consciousness by illustrating the premise that changes needed to be made within the Church for it to become more Christ-like. Cranach used the second element of a political cartoon, in the context of a widely recognised story or setting, to get his point across.

Caricature goes back to Leonardo da Vinci's artistic explorations of 'the ideal type of deformity' (the grotesque), which he used to improve the understanding of the concept of ideal beauty. He found his models of inspiration in the poor areas of cities such as Milan. From the beginning caricatures have been linked with social and economical events.

In the Low Countries, artists like Hieronymus Bosch and Peter Brueghel the Elder used caricatures to give more expression to their main themes. Caricatures were linked with evil, the devil, and the dark side of life (De Bruyne, 1940). Intended to be light-hearted satires, their caricatures were in essence a form of counter-art. A new style developed, of quick, impressionistic drawing, that exaggerated prominent physical characteristics with the intention of creating a humorous effect.

Thomas Nast, a nineteenth century German migrant to America, created some of the earliest political cartoons. He became famous for the first visual depiction of Santa Claus in the form in which he is currently shown. He also published a series of cartoons targeting corruption in government, and the resulting public outcry became intolerable for politicians. His accusations against the politician, William Marcy Tweed, led Tweed to retort 'Let's stop those damned pictures. I don't care so much what the papers write about me – my constituents can't read but damn it, they can see pictures.' As a result of Nast's campaign the politician was arrested for corruption. Nast later exerted a strong influence on politics through his cartoons and engravings, which included the Republican elephant and the Democratic donkey. But since that period, cartoon art has been perceived as an oxymoron or a contradiction.

The following comment was found in the guestbook of an annual international exhibition of cartoons (www.cartoonfestival.be):

> A cartoonist is the professional joker in a castle with kings and queens, with ministers and spies. The joker developed campaigns against indifference, the experience of contrast. His battlefield is paper; his ammunition words and pictures; his howitzers are printing presses, the newspapers and the magazines, sometimes a textbook for children.

The twenty edited books of the best cartoons (Toerisme Knokke-Heist, 1983-2004) show that each cartoonist stands for a particular concept of life, shaped by people who have built a nation dedicated to enduring principles. Cartoons suggest aspects of national and international life that are bad. The reader is given a particular point of view – *couleur locale* – of citizenship, linked to 'war, sexuality, poverty, environment problems, care, disability, racism.'

When the cartoonist transcribes scenes to paper he (usually 'he') naturally represents neither their shapes nor the colours as they actually appear, but he swirls his brush into agitated rhythms and colour-contrasts which express his moods and feelings. After 9/11 I used the daily cartoons by the famous American cartoonist, Clay Bennett (www.clay bennett.com), and by two Belgians, GAL and Marec, to develop philosophical discussions on fear, prejudice, racism, intolerance, security, the American way of life and Islam. Before I came to the classroom I read the headlines and comments on the internet (www. truthout.org) and my students collected oral remarks from their locality. For more than a month we worked on this clash (Verkest, 2002). Cartoons became an important medium of communication for my students and they used them in their courses on world orientation and current affairs. They see cartoons as an essential element in the world of newspapers and political talk shows – although in education, they still have a marginal role.

Today cartoon art may be dismissed by academics, corporate leaders and politicians, who claim cartoons cannot possibly be art, that they are not much more than entertainment for children. But cartoon art acts as a bridge between those who want 'just the facts' and those who look for relationships with other, hidden, facts. Using cartoons enables one to get the whole class into a creative mindset, engendering the kind of philosophical talk teachers do not usually expect from students. For the cartoonist, the individual citizen is sometimes needs to be alerted to the reality of the situation. He or she may be incapable of acting critically, cannot come to any judgement about relationships and makes platitudinous pronouncements (Verkest, 2001).

The role of the teacher in using cartoons

What kind of teacher is needed to use art and cartoons in this way? Three possible pedagogic models are suggested by Bulckens (1997, 2003). The first of these can be demonstrated as a triangle. The base of the triangle is the subject matter and the pupil: the top is dominated by the teacher, who looks on the pupils as empty vessels or *tabula rasa*. The teacher fills them up with knowledge and asks yes/no questions. There is no room left for difference: this is an example of a monologue.

In the second model, pupils and teacher set off together on an adventure. It is not the teacher's knowledge that takes the lead but the abundant experiences of the group itself. The teacher is only a pacemaker, driving the learning process but remaining in the background. The teacher, familiar with group dynamics and social skills, leads the way to the discovery of new worlds and perspectives. Pupils and the teacher may bring new ideas to the learning process and look at the subject material from the same perspective. In doing so, they examine a painting and interpret it together. This leads to a new role for the teacher: s/he becomes a facilitator and moderator in working with art or cartoons. This model has a structure based on commitment.

In the third model the teacher tries to support children and young people to develop themselves through contact with others and at the same time with other realities. In this model we find a trialogue. The teacher helps the class group to appropriate intellectual patrimony and religious heritage actively, constructively and creatively (Antone and Mortier, 1997). Children look for visual data and, in collaboration with other children and the teacher, they investigate and organise critical talk.

Two sources of inspiration for the critical discussion

This idea of using cartoons as a tool for critical thinking comes from the work of Paulo Freire, the Brazilian popular educator who used it successfully in classes and workshops. Freire taught literacy to peasants through the pictures they made of daily events, drawings that provided material that students could use to reflect on economics, politics, and relationships of power. Freire imparted literacy and *conscientization*: an explicit awareness of the political nature of personal troubles. His pedagogy is grounded largely in the adult literacy programme he directed in rural Brazil. In 1964, a coup led to the military regime that halted his work because of its 'subversive' nature.

Freire's pedagogy assumes that learners already have valuable experiences which are the starting point for education. In his view learners are not, as in the traditional education model, analogous to banks, where teachers deposit information and at the end of the semester ask for their deposits back with added interest. Instead Freire offers an image of education as a dialogue, in which teachers and learners examine the details of life's experiences as they acquire new information and develop new skills of reflection. Freire's methods are useful in helping literate people communicate their ideas more concisely, allowing all members of a group a chance to express themselves.

In the 1970s the American philosopher, Mathew Lipman, was disappointed by the teaching methods at University. Students were not able to think by themselves. He investigated whether it was possible to stimulate young children's development through lessons in philosophy and critical thinking. He initiated the Institute for Advancement of Philosophy for Children, and wrote books for children which set out some of his philosophical ideas. In the early 1990s Lipman's *Philosophy for children* (P4C) was adapted and translated into Dutch by Berrie Heesen (1996), who started a 'Centre of Philosophy for Children', only partly realised before he died in 2002. Pupils who think critically for themselves are not the easiest to teach, though they are unlikely to be, intentionally, disruptive to the whole class. The process of initiating a community of inquiry is based on democratic principles and commitments, making each child's contribution to the discussion of equal value. A community of inquiry often works best when an outsider joins the group to facilitate inquiry, because in the early stages children may expect their teacher to answer questions and may feel unable to discuss things with them.

The combination of critical thinking and art allow pupils to co-operate as a learning community (Brenifier, 2001). By so doing, teachers avoid ignorant and stereotyped patterns of argument, tart comments and cynicism (Brenifier, 2002b). By integrating children's' initiation to citizenship with philosophical thinking, citizenship education moves away from being a collection of data about the functions of the state and political institutions. Education in citizenship, based on Socratic or critical dialogues (Saran and Neisser, 2004), starts with a concrete visual experience and encourages children to ask questions about controversial issues (Brenifier, 2002a). Critical thinking creates a positive sense of citizenship because children reach an agreement about the aims of their thinking together and achieve common ways of interpretation. Last but not least, children agree on central pre-suppositions about different ways of thinking and discussing. The more open the way in which questions are formulated and the less they are based on pre-suppositions, the more they will encourage pupils to be free-thinking (Gronke, 2001).

The new role of cartoons in combination with P4C

In relation to learning, the use of cartoons has two major advantages:

- Cartoons are highly memorable. This is because they create a state of relaxed receptivity, and because their messages touch deep-seated emotional or aesthetic needs. Like songs, cartoons stick in the head.

- They are highly motivating, especially for children, adolescents, and young adult learners. Cartoons and comics in their many forms constitute a powerful sub-culture with its own 'priesthood'.

It would not make sense to ignore this flexible and attractive resource: history, civic education and religious education have always made good use of cartoons. Anything you can do with a text you can do with a cartoon: the use of cartoons gets everyone on the same wavelength, creates common goals and terminology and makes formal modelling much easier, faster and more accurate. Concepts such as identity and a sense of public responsibility can be visualised in this way. Using cartoons, we are able to create various environments and instruments that facilitate discussion and dialogue.

The lack of cartoons in textbooks

Looking in recent textbooks for children it can be seen that there are more and more pictures, most of which only illustrate the stories. When students completed a questionnaire about the pictures in these textbooks, only 23 per cent of questions were about the pictures.

Only religious textbooks contained extra information about the pictures and a checklist of questions. We looked through twenty new textbooks for the age group nine to twelve years of age, which were edited between 1998 and 2003, and we found only 23 cartoons. Only eight cartoons were analysed in the exercise book. Few publishers work with this material. In interviews with authors and editors, most stated that they were unfamiliar with this approach. One class of students conducted an experiment. Half of the class made an ordinary worksheet and included a picture in it, while the other group used two cartoons. There was more intense, and longer, discussion over selecting the cartoons than the picture. They included the picture at a later stage in the process, and left themselves no time to explore the visual data (Verkest, 2004).

It is essential to teach children how to use cartoons. Cartoons are sometimes confused with comics, which are also worth using in school. Comics should not only be used to promote particular values, but to show interaction between people, optimism about life, and can offer alternative solutions to specific emergencies. The artist wants to distinguish himself from others who want to express and stimulate pleasure without interest. The 'picture stuck in my head' phenomenon also seems to reinforce the idea that images work on both our short and long term memory.

The combination of art with humour creates bosom companions. Humour is said to be the marriage of ideas and images which had not previously been seen to be related to each other. Cartoons are usually composed of two elements: caricature, which parodies the individual, and allusion, which creates the context into which the individual is placed. Cartoons can possess an emancipatory potential: they are based on a grammar of illustration that links visual elements with the potential effects on the reader.

Taking cartoons to the classroom

Looking at what we do with cartoons outside the classroom, and then at what we might do with them in class, may reveal ways of exploiting them. We can draws up a checklist for the teacher and the pupils to use to look more closely at an image (see the end of this chapter). However, we must be careful not to kill the material by making the activity seem like serious work. Children recognise that some cartoons are just for fun, whilst others convey shocking meanings.

Working with cartoons, we learn both about children and from children, letting them choose and explain their choice of cartoons. They can design exercises for their classmates, which gives them active control over and responsibility for their own learning. Students are often content to be passive watchers: teachers should encourage student interaction with cartoons, and invite them to predict, describe and share their perceptions.

We can ask children what objects they see in the cartoons (Kress, 1996). Certain objects are common to cartooning: they are a vocabulary list, as in the checklist below. Children can suggest why some of these objects appear so frequently. In this way, they learn to recognise and comprehend symbols, and what they represent. It would be interesting to choose a symbol from a cartoon and to ask three different people what it represents. They could choose people of different ages, such as parents or grandparents, as well as of gender and background to look at the chosen cartoon. Pupils will appreciate the importance of current events through investigating cartoons. Cartoons can be categorised on several levels, such as mankind, space, time, religion, technique, environment, society and sexuality.

Cartoons can be linked to the news in magazines and the papers, and to current or historic situations. In one class a large circle was divided into several segments, in each of which the teacher put 'hot issues', and then decided with the children whether the news items were local, regional, national or international. The teacher used pictures and also an editorial cartoon from a newspaper: pupils were able to see that the regional element had been influenced by the national and the European level.

A practical example

The cartoon shown below was used in a local environmental project undertaken with students in a Freinetschool in 2001, when there was a debate over the destruction of a green zone in the neighbourhood of the school. A Flemish cartoonist created a set of cartoons on this topic, and allowed one cartoon to be used with the class. The humour in cartoons can increase awareness of a conflict. It can even help to reduce and restrain the stress involved in a 'civic conflict'. Cartoons may encourage deliberation, and help children and teachers to see different points of view of the same situation (Amir, 2004).

This cartoonist's work often makes use of binary oppositions, the most important of which are:

nature – civilisation

brute force – domestic order

lack of control – excessive intervention

role of alternative movements – role of government and market forces

health and prosperity – sickness and disease

realism – idealism

perspective of cartoonist – perspective of the actor

Using a framework of paired oppositions, the students examined editorial cartoons which specifically targeted the current civic situation.

Three themes were selected:

- The representation of a political, social or economical situation as an entity, an object or a person, which in this case was two men playing a game of draughts with trees and apartment blocks. After analysing the cartoon children make a list of 'meta-questions', which are open and reflective questions which make clear that children are putting forward their own perspectives. These questions should be seen as an offer to other pupils to ask yet more questions from their own perspective.

  Some examples: What would be the rules in this game? Who is responsible for the rules? How are they controlled? What is the target of the rules? In your opinion, what is forbidden in the game? Do they need an arbitrator? Who may have won or lost by the game? Is this game an aggressive one? Is this game leisure for these checkers players?

- The presence of the state or the policy represented in the cartoon. Children are able to answer 'perspective-oriented questions' which suggested different perspectives from which questions could be formulated: 'If you put yourself in his place, what would you think then?'

  Some examples: What is more important: trees or apartments? Have trees got rights? Can trees be sacrificed for apartments? When do trees beat apartments? How could you 'win' an apartment? Which draught player would you support? Can people defend trees? Are these men good citizens? Are they fair? How would you describe their citizenship?

- The way the cartoon works to generate humour through the opening up of positions of relative epistemological advantage. That is, the cartoonist and the reader have a more informed perspective on the state of the regional or national economy or socio-political situation, which the characters in it do not have. The policy shown in the example is that of a hard player destroying nature, and another player, representing the environmental movement trying to stop the expansion of the built area.

  Some examples: Has the cartoonist forgotten anything? What would you add? How do you feel when you look at this drawing? Do you consider this to be a cartoon? What made you laugh? Which other opposite objects could you find for playing draughts? Is this the best way (to play and to be silent) to solve the problem? Do you know who is at the table? What is his function? Are they able to talk to each other or do they like to play in silence? Do they trust each other? Does the cartoonist think that we are free agents, or that our actions are determined by others? What forces does the cartoonist suggest are behind what is going on?

After the critical discussion, the eleven year-old pupils enjoyed this cartoon and wrote stories about it, starting with text balloons from the figures. The core questions were: what are they thinking and what are they dreaming? When seen as fun, it can be easy to explain difficult ideas concerning citizenship. Cartoon art is a powerful way to talk about difficult and scary issues. But sometimes cartoons are no more than illustrations which substitute for the lack of awareness of current events in their readers. This sustains the prejudice that pictures are only for children. Due to the cartoon, pupils tried to find the people in charge of plans and made a list of several questions and statements based on the philosophical discussion which had taken place.

The teacher put together several proverbs concerning playing, trees, power, play, citizenship. He not only collected and explained but also critically evaluated the proverbs. Pupils wrote letters and asked for an interview with people from the local environmental group, the deputy for environment, the mayor and the project development manager. By making it public in the local press the discussion got started and plans were made. This approach was based on the idea that normally both teachers and pupils fail to engage in participatory and active senses of citizenship (*'un manque du sentiment de citoyenneté'*, Brenifier, 2002a)

People often fail to recognise the validity of visual learning, and believe that it is for less intelligent people to resort to – this is an attitude that should not be sustained in light of the available evidence. Fortunately, this viewpoint is changing, particularly as the television generation reaches maturity and begins to re-define culture norms.

The best way of using a cartoon is as an introduction to a theme, before the project begins, or to illustrate and reinforce what has already been discussed. Children and teachers should realise that a cartoon is just a kind of snapshot, and that discussing it must include placing it in context: this means considering what happened before, and at the moment the cartoon was created. I generally avoid cartoons with a verbal discourse or with text balloons, because these tend to undermine the idea of conveying meaning through the technique of delicate drawing. Cartoons are thoughtfully composed with great attention to detail. They can be used to enhance, to reinforce or as centre-pieces in lessons such as civic education or world orientation.

Checklist for using cartoons

Who are the main figures in this cartoon?

Which figures have a subordinate function?

What is he or she wearing?

Where are the figures? Can you guess?

What is the background?

What expression is on the person's face?

Is the person moving, standing, sitting?

Which figures have an active or an executive function?

Which figures could you easily identity with?

Who takes the important decisions?

Are there any real people in the cartoon? Who is portrayed in the cartoon?

What problem is illustrated by the cartoon?

Who solves the problem? How is the problem solved?

Are there any positive or negative associations with this topic? What are the colours?

What is actually said? Are the words insulting? Are they shocking?

Do the words add anything to the picture?

What information is given about this issue?

Can you tell cartoonist's point of view from the cartoon?

What is the cartoonist's opinion about the topic portrayed in the cartoon?

Do you agree or disagree with the cartoonist's opinion? Why?

Are there symbols in the cartoon? What are they and what do they represent?

Teachers can ask small groups or pairs of students to 'read' the cartoon and to create discussion questions based on the cartoon or arising from its main themes. Each group can then write their best question on the blackboard or a flipchart, so that the teacher can use it in the second part of the lesson. Before the teacher starts philosophical questioning, it is important to note the similarities and differences in the questions from different groups. The class might rank the questions they find most interesting.

Some teachers have collected not just good stories but also paintings and 'committed' cartoons about social and ecological issues, about handling conflict, bullying, virtues and emotions. Any of these can spark off discussions. A lively discussion should follow the questionnaire and teachers are often amazed at how well children react to the cartoons that have been displayed.

In a world of global civilisation, only those who are looking for a technical trick to save civilisation need feel despair. But those who believe in the mysterious power of their own human 'being', which mediates between them and the mysterious power of the 'world being', have no reason to despair at all (Havel, 1994).

11

A diverse learning community: the role of continuing professional development

Maggie Ross

S taff development plays a key role in any professional approach to implementing change, whether it is the result of government curriculum initiatives, structuring of services or changes in the local population of users. For English practitioners recent developments have included new guidance for working with children under three, the expansion of early childhood provision that includes a move towards 'children's centres' where families can expect to access a wider range of services such as health, family support and social services, some adult education provision and advice on returning to or entering employment; and demands for an expanded and better qualified workforce to meet this expansion. In London, as in other parts of the country, the community is ethnically, culturally and linguistically diverse and communities using early years settings may change fairly rapidly. Practitioners need to meet these changes with a commitment to equality of access for all children and adults. In London settings the staff group frequently reflects the diversity in the community to some degree. Nursery staff from minority ethnic groups form eight per cent of the workforce, and 32 per cent of the workforce in London (Surestart, 2004). There is an imbalance in that there are fewer staff from minority ethnic communities in higher levels of pay and status. Diversity is both a potential strength and a challenge. Staff knowledge and experience may be strong in terms of potential response to the needs of a diverse community of children and parents. Staff development, on the other hand, must recognise that all staff are entitled to training for equal opportunities practice and that it is essential that opportunities exist for all staff to develop successful career paths. This chapter explores some aspects of a learning community in early childhood practice, focusing on a group of early childhood staff working with 50 young children, from six moths to five years of age, and their parents, at a time of considerable change in the demands placed on them by outside agencies.

Membership of a community, with rights and responsibilities, starts early. The youngest members of this early childhood setting are only six months old, but from the start young children are members of the family and community groups into which they are born and from the earliest days of a child's life learning about self and group begin (Trevarthen, 1998; Rogoff, 1990). It is important that any nursery or pre-school setting demonstrates respect for individual and family identity, in terms of ethnicity, culture, language, individual strengths and needs. In London the diverse community and the movements of groups and individuals within it, mean that most practitioners work with children from a range of communities. They will frequently need to respond, as professionals, to a wide range of families, ensuring recognition of different experience, understanding different values and expectations in relation to childcare and early education. We know that very young children learn the reactions and responses to difference from those who care for them (Brown, 1998) and that these are demonstrated both through explicit references and implicit behaviours.

Staffing structure and qualifications
Early childhood practitioners in England come from a range of training levels. There are qualified early years teachers, working almost exclusively with children over three years old mostly in state provision, some early childhood educators who usually have qualifications in early childhood education and care which are equivalent to degree entry and others who have a lower level qualification which

is at school leaving level. Within local authority provision most staff have degree entry level qualifications and increasingly some of these staff hold, or are working towards, a degree in early childhood studies. Nationally, all training for early childhood qualifications, including teaching standards, requires students to understand the importance of equality of opportunity for both children and families. Inspection frameworks also review this aspect of a setting's work. However, not all settings currently meet this requirement equally or even well.

Practice guidance and the early years curriculum

Curriculum and practice guidance for young children makes specific reference to equal opportunities. In England new guidance for those working with children under three years old is now in place (Surestart, 2002). This guidance is not a curriculum for young children, but is intended to offer a framework for practice to ensure that all children who are cared for outside their homes will receive standards of care that enable them to develop well, making good progress across all areas of development. The guidance sets out four aspects: a strong child, a skilful communicator, a competent learner and a healthy child.

For children from three to six there is a curriculum. The guidance for the foundation stage (DfEE, 2000) allows considerable freedom in terms of how staff plan their work with children, but has quite stringent requirements that children should work towards specific goals that most are expected to meet by the end of the first year of formal schooling, at the age of five to six years old. Steps leading to these goals are described across six areas of the curriculum: personal, social and emotional development, communication, language and literacy, mathematical development, knowledge and understanding of the world, physical development and creative development.

Both these documents include statements about the importance of practices that respect, and reflect, individual children's differences. However, it is only in the curriculum guidance for children from three years onwards that a statement specifically addressing the importance of equality of access appears in the opening statements of

151

principle 'No child should be excluded or disadvantaged because of ethnicity, culture or religion, home language, family background, special educational needs, disability, gender or ability' (DfEE, 2000, p11).

Diversity in the staff group and in the community of families

At the early years setting that is the focus of this chapter staff come from different ethnic and cultural backgrounds. In a staff group of twenty people, ten are from Black African or Black Caribbean backgrounds, some having come to the UK as adults, others were born and brought up in the UK. Three staff have come to the UK from other European countries. There are also staff from Greek Cypriot and Turkish Cypriot backgrounds who have grown up in the UK. Eight staff in total are from white European backgrounds. Twelve languages including English are spoken fluently, many by more than one staff member. Half of the staff speak at least two languages fluently. Although this is a staff group with particularly diverse backgrounds it is not exceptional in London. Staff backgrounds do not mirror the backgrounds of the children who attend the setting, but the range of backgrounds is in many ways similar. Thirty per cent of the children attending the centre speak another language in addition to English, and currently the number of families where parents do not speak English fairly confidently is quite small. A significant but small number of children enter the nursery at two or three years old without previous experience of English.

Developing practice in response to central guidance

With the guidance and curriculum documents in place, staff at the centre plan their work in teams to reflect the strengths and needs of children in the groups they work with. There are both teaching staff who work principally in the room with children over three, and early childhood educators who have a qualification at diploma level. Many of these staff hold or are working towards degree qualifications or above. Essentially, planning discussions take place at both whole centre meetings (training days and staff meetings), team meetings of staff working with a group of children, and in meetings to with parents.

Initial meetings with parents are an opportunity to become informed about individual children's family experience and individual needs, and subsequent discussions with parents continue to play a crucial role (Siraj-Blatchford and Clarke, 2000). Providing opportunities for parents to contribute to work at the centre also leads into changes in ways of working with children and supports the development of staff skills and knowledge. This may arise through a specifically chosen focus that will enable staff to respond more effectively to the experience of all children, such as when a bilingual parent may contribute specific skills in terms of reading or telling stories in a community language, or a parent may share particular knowledge, such as cooking or music making from a specific cultural group. Such initiatives also ensure that the curriculum is not restricted to the majority group experience, or dependent on the knowledge of current staff members. Building a broader profile of children's experiences is essential if we are to understand what children already know so that we can more effectively reflect, and respect, their lives and support their progress (Kenner, 2000; Brown, 1998).

Team planning works from the basis of observations of children, looking at dispositions and attitudes (Carr, 2001; Dowling, 2001) as well as knowledge and skills. The guidance for children under three (Surestart, 2002) is a fairly open document, allowing for a responsive approach to children. The curriculum guidance for over threes is much more tightly structured. An approach that responds to individual children's strengths and needs can be harder to achieve unless staff feel confident about their ability to address the 'goals' for children, through a curriculum that is responsive and open to change. In observations and in assessments undertaken, it is important that staff have the ability to recognise the differences in individual children and their varied family and community experiences in order to make sense of what they are observing (Ross, 2001). Value judgements can be masked as professionally competent assessments unless we are careful to examine our own knowledge base and are aware of our own prejudice (Brown, 1998; Lane, 1998). Despite the

153

statements in everyone of our guidance documents there is a danger that practice remains tokenistic and superficial. The examples of practice given in the guidance are not always strong examples of an approach that recognises and values the breadth and depth of diversity in our community: staff need to be constantly aware of this (Nieto, 1999).

Drawing on the experience of staff from diverse backgrounds

Team work in early years settings is a source of strength. Because of the nature of work with young children it is usual for staff to work closely together, sharing the care and education of the group , and also their knowledge about these children. The work is a complex mixture of emotional, physical, social and intellectual care, demanding social, emotional, physical and intellectual skills of adults. The very complexity of the relationship between care and education may allow staff to see children's needs in ways that are not as easy for teachers working with older children for whom the prime focus may be intellectual. The primary need to recognise and support children's developing sense of themselves, so that they are able to grow in strength and confidence, means that it is essential for staff to respond with an open and honest appreciation of diversity throughout all aspects of care and education (ECEF, 1998).

Having colleagues who come from different ethnic, cultural, linguistic, social and religious backgrounds is a very special resource, because role models are offered for children, support for parents and professional support for the staff group. Staff strengths may range from the ability to speak to a child in her home language to give her comfort as she goes to sleep, or familiarity with childcare patterns and knowledge of important personal aspects of a child's life such as skin or hair care, to an understanding of the complex relationships those from minority ethnic groups experience in Britain, and the effects of the often nuanced prejudice met in daily life (Nieto, 1999).

However, staff experience is not in itself sufficient, nor does it necessarily lead to effective practice. Staff discussion and learning is as important for a diverse staff group as for a homogenous one. For the early years setting described here staff development has taken place through different routes.

Access to further education and training

There are a number of different courses available to staff at the centre, including both in- service training courses that demand no specific previous experience and do not generally contribute to qualifications, and training and education courses at both pre-degree, degree and postgraduate level. Some of these courses are run by the local area's education service, but most by colleges or universities and are taught, work-based or distance learning courses. The local university and further education colleges support innovative access routes into education for adults who may not have traditional educational qualifications. These routes are important for many of those working in early childhood education where for so long there has been an assumption that this is a career that did not need academic qualifications. For our staff group, from a range of different educational backgrounds, this provision has been key to opening up staff development possibilities.

The drive to support equality of access to higher education for groups of students who have not traditionally been well represented in higher education has resulted in the creation of strong learning groups in the local university and a student body that reflects the diversity of London's population. It also means that expectations of the kind of support new students may need is realistic, and that study skills are often offered at the start of courses, as is ongoing access to help with academic writing. For students who are writing academic essays in their second language this is of great importance. Staff in the early years service are clear about the opportunities that this provides.

It is also important that our local council has a firm commitment to staff development in general and especially to its early years service. Staff have part of their fees refunded on successful completion of the modules taken. The centre has funded the remainder of the fees for the first two-thirds of degree courses, in recognition of the fact that the cost of the modules can be prohibitive when staff are on relatively low incomes and this in itself would be against the ethos of equal access to success.

These commitments to equality, in the design of entry routes to university or college and throughout the courses, are crucial to being able to offer an experience of inclusive education to staff. Staff returning to work at the centre, following an evening lecture where they feel their own experiences are valued, are positive about their roles in developing inclusive practice. Certainly there is well-articulated discussion among staff when they are encouraging colleagues to take up study. There is a sense of future possibilities and a realistic assessment of what is needed in terms of initial preparation and support. Honest descriptions are shared, of how if feels at the beginning when everything is new, how hard it can be to feel confident to contribute to discussion in an unfamiliar group and how difficult the process of writing can be. Staff have chosen courses that both reflect their professional interests in continuing to work in early childhood education and allow them to progress to higher educational qualifications that have intrinsic value as well as a specific application in terms of career development.

Practice related courses: the importance of relevance and reflective practice

Most although not all of the courses chosen by staff have a strong practice-related element, although only the work-based route into teaching has a specific practice assessment. All but one of the college and university courses studied have clearly articulated aims to address equal opportunities. These aims are reflected across all modules; there are also a number of modules that focus on specific equality themes: a degree level module that looks at work with bilingual children and another that specifically addresses issues of inclusive practice. Recent research into effective practice in early childhood provision has highlighted the importance of inclusive curriculum approaches (Siraj-Blatchford et al., 2004).

Course assessment draws heavily on reflective practice which both enables staff to review their own practice and requires them to share the ideas they are exploring with their colleagues. Examples of specific projects developed by staff are:

- creating books in English and Turkish for a bilingual child, working closely with a parent and a Turkish-speaking colleague at the centre

- looking at early literacy experiences, including the experiences of young children from a range of cultural and linguistic backgrounds

- looking at developing health awareness in young children, which includes awareness of different diets and eating patterns.

At the completion of an assessment project the work continues: in each case we have gained not only greater knowledge but an awareness of where our weaknesses lie.

There are no assumptions that bilingual staff understand the needs of all bilingual children, but there is an understanding that they have a depth of understanding about language which monolingual staff do not posses. When the staff group consider different approaches to childcare, personal experiences are shared and reflected upon which can be drawn on in the work situation. Staff themselves say that the opportunity to discuss, read, reflect and to have to prepare oral presentations and essays has developed their thinking, their professional competence and their confidence. The language of team meetings and staff training days is changing rapidly, and new staff are drawn into this practice of discussing their work with colleagues. There is a real sharing of experience and support for one another, which has also affected our work with parents.

Working with parents

Meetings are held for parents about the curriculum of the centre and about issues concerning childcare and being a parent. Parents are aware of training days being held at the centre, which is common practice in such a setting. Information about the focus of training is shared in newsletters and in general conversations. When they enrol their child at the centre parents are asked if they are willing for photographs to be used for a range of purposes, one of which is as material for study. They are also made aware of the topics studied by individual members of staff. This information is shared through individual conversations, such as to explain why team members may be absent on a course, or when a parent is asked for permission to use material relating to an individual child. Another important kind of conversation is the social interaction that takes place between staff and parents at the beginnings and end of the day. Staff are open to parents in many ways: they share discussions about what their work involves and about how they are developing their practice through study. The primary intentions of our commitment to staff development have been to develop better practices with children and to support staff in pursuing qualifications and developing their careers. Another outcome has been to provide support for parents' learning.

The centre has had a number of parents working on a volunteer basis with children: this is common practice in many settings. Staff discussion of their current study has supported parents who are considering formal training, at various levels, and these parents become part of the community of learners. This explicit initiative on parents' education reflects the national focus on changing things for families by helping parents to move into, or back into work and thereby towards greater economic security.

Support systems

Informal relationships provide most of the 'mentoring' that supports individual staff. There is a strong sense of the apprenticeship model of learning between staff, echoing elements of our approach to children's learning (Rogoff, 1990). Staff who have moved forward in their studies are generous in both encouragement and ongoing support of colleagues. Reading material is shared and course work discussed at length; support is offered when assignments are written. There is now a good staff library and use of computers at the centre, plus a laptop that can be borrowed for home use. Staff who are competent at using information technology support those who are less so. I am often asked for informal tutorial time and this has been a joy, listening to staff reflecting on their practice in the light of study.

The high number of staff now studying has meant that it is accepted across the centre that there will always need to be flexibility in working patterns so that colleagues are able to leave in time for evening courses. Staff study at the centre at the beginning or end of their shifts and during lunch breaks, and the centre can be used on Saturdays where it provides peace and quiet, a library and computer access.

Courses undertaken range from initial qualification to post-graduate level, and this means that the learning community is inclusive of all. If there were only support for initial training we would be disenfranchising staff who wish to progress to leadership and management roles in early childhood education. It is essential for this to be possible so that the work force at every level will reflect the diverse community of children and practitioners.

Contact with European colleagues

For the past two years we have been very fortunate to have had contact with colleagues in Copenhagen, Denmark, through an EU funded LEONARDO project. Three social pedagogue students from Copenhagen have each completed a six-month placement at the centre, and two more students are starting. The focus of their work in this placement is working with diverse communities. This emphasis has meant that we have had to look at our work differently, explaining our structures and practice to colleagues from another European background. We have had to be articulate about our strengths as well as weaknesses. Because we are aware of the need for better inclusive practice we do not always acknowledge what we already do well, both in terms of national and local provision and in our own setting. Our link with Denmark has caused us to think about the diversity of our staff group, and how we use the expertise among it that we may take for granted, and perhaps sometimes fail to use as effectively as we might.

The individual Danish students have contributed their own perspectives and experiences to our work, challenging us in terms of the more structured UK curriculum for young children and learning from our work with families and our approaches to ethnic and cultural diversity and bilingualism. For all of them it is a new experience to work with colleagues from so many different ethnic groups and with staff from African and Caribbean backgrounds in leading roles.

Staff as trainers

The centre has taken students from local colleges and universities for a long time, and this has continued as staff move on in their studies. The level of supervision of students has increased as staff discuss the theories behind their practice more confidently and reflect on their work more analytically. Students who come to the centre are from a range of backgrounds and it is a positive experience for them to be aware that the staff group is involved in on-going training. This offers students an opportunity to talk about their own career after initial training. Students have access to the library and to computer facilities at the centre and the staff offer considerable help with study. Individual members of staff have also become involved in training in the local area, working on courses for those employed to look after children in their homes. They have taught on modules which are about building relationships with parents and implementing equal opportunities. Four staff members have visited Denmark to look at early childhood provision and to lead seminars at our partner institution.

Some conclusions

Staff interaction with colleagues in the centre and with students on their courses has an important influence on the development of a strong learning community. Our drive towards inclusive practice that treats all children and families equally is supported by courses that also reinforce these aims. Staff need role models in tutors who keep this inclusive practice at the centre of their work and need to feel confident to challenge tutors, or fellow students or colleagues who are not so committed to equality.

The group has something particularly strong to offer to practice in this inner London community. This comes, I am sure, from its diversity in terms of ethnicity, language, culture and religion. If staff are fully committed to equality for all young children and families, in terms of both their feelings of acceptance in the setting, and access to a curriculum that is both respectful and appropriately challenging for all children, we need to accept the degree to which are own beliefs and values pay a large part in our work.

> What happens in classrooms is first and foremost about the personal and collective connections that exist among the individuals who inhabit those spaces. Consequently, teachers' beliefs and values, how these are communicated to students through teaching practices and behaviours, and their impact on the lives of students – these are the factors that make teaching so consequential in the lives of many people. (Nieto, 1999, p130)

In early childhood settings the teaching also involves patterns of care and nurturing, and relationships with parents and other family members need to be close and reciprocal.

Nieto suggests that educators need to pay most attention to their own growth and transformation and the 'lives, realities, and dreams of their students' (*ibid,* p131). All staff working towards better understandings of equality can offer role models for children and indeed for parents, but a strong staff group, which represents the diversity of the community it serves, is both a positive role model for children and a rich resource for its own learning. For each of us in the centre there is the advantage of a diverse peer group within which to learn. 'The process of transformation is a personal and collective journey that teachers must travel' (*ibid,* p131).

Reflecting on developments which have taken place over the past three years, some aspects stand out.

• It has been of utmost importance to have access to training for staff without traditional school qualifications, including routes into higher education for experienced staff without formal academic qualifications

• The focus on equal opportunities within the courses studied and the local in-service education provided is of great importance

- The development of a strong ethos of the importance of training has meant that individuals can expect support from all colleagues across the centre

- The apprenticeship model of learning has been central to this success. Sharing learning 'alongside' is what gives confidence to individuals and means that everything we do is a joint enterprise feeding into our shared work at the centre for the children

- The opportunity to work with colleagues from elsewhere in Europe has enabled us to reflect on diversity in a broader context

- Parents have been very supportive of staff. An understanding from staff that parents are also members of the learning community leads to valuable exchanges about learning, about different routes into training and possible career development for parents as well as staff. A diverse staff learning community demonstrates that achievement is not the preserve of one particular ethnic group

- The possibility of career advancement: some staff have moved on to other work requiring the degree level work they have embarked on at the centre, others have taken on new responsibilities at the centre. There is an ongoing conversation about career progression

- A staff group that is in itself a 'learning resource' that we have all been able to draw on. And the generosity of individual members so that colleagues feel confident to explore what are sometimes difficult and challenging areas in an atmosphere of trust, allowing prejudices to be unlearnt.

This work is not new, but practitioners from ethnic minority groups are still under-represented in our field: this is particularly true at management level. We believe that this matters to children, to families and to practitioners. Staff development should have equality and inclusion at its centre, and should be accessible to all. Children growing up in Europe will be members of an increasingly diverse community: their education in early childhood needs to be led by those who can respect and reflect this diversity.

162

Notes on Contributors

Anne-Marie Dinvaut is a teacher of English and a teacher trainer for the pedagogy of languages and cultures in the IUFM of Lyon (France). Her particular research interests include exploring the potential of pupils and teachers in the teaching of foreign languages. She works with the ICAR (*Interaction Corpus Apprentissages Représentations*) and ADIS-LST (*Apprentissages, Discours Interactions – Savoirs linguistiques, scientifiques et techniques laboratories*), Sciences du Langage, Université Lumière, Lyon.

Kristín Dýrfjörd has been an assistant professor at the University of Akureyri (Iceland), Faculty of Education since 1997. Her specialist field is early childhood studies and the external evaluation of schools. She was leader of a pre-school in Iceland for nine years before she became a teacher in a new department for Early Childhood Studies at the University, where she participated in developing these new studies. As a head teacher, her school was one of the first Icelandic pre-schools to participate in a European project. She was on the Ministry of Education committee that wrote the 1999 National curriculum for pre-schools. Her main research interests are democracy in pre-schools, working with under threes, and the evaluation of pre-schools.

Maria Luísa Freitas is associate professor of Social Studies Education at the Institute of Child Studies at the University of Minho (Portugal). She teaches initial and in-service courses in elementary and childhood teacher education. The focus of her research interests is on how children develop time and space concepts, as well as identity and citizenship in the context of social studies classrooms in primary schools. In her most recent publications she emphasises the connections between citizenship education and cooperative learning.

Yveline Fumat is professor emeritus at Université Paul Valéry Montpellier III in the south of France. She was initially a primary school teacher, and following her *Agrégée de Philosophie* became a secondary teacher. Moving to work at University, she taught *Philosophie morale et*

163

politique. Her research about political and social education, particularly for younger children, and her interest in national guidelines for *Ecole maternelle* underlie her interest in this chapter.

Søren Hegstrup is the head of the Department for Development and Research at Hindholm University College (Denmark). His research interests are educational policy and sociology. At the moment he is engaged in a three-year research project on *BA thesis* in cooperation with the University of Roskilde. Other projects are democracy and solidarity in university colleges. He is a member of the CiCe steering group

Aili Helenius is a professor of early childhood education at the University of Turku, Department of Teacher Education in Rauma (Finland). Her research topics are the development of play and imagination in the early childhood, especially the first three years of development. Her recent publications and presentations have focused on cultural and historical themes. She has led an Interreg II Karelian project on the early communicative development and multiculturalism supported by the European Social Fund.

Riitta Korhonen is a senior lecturer at the University of Turku in the Department of Teacher Education in Rauma (Finland). She lectures on teaching in pre-school and primary education and on special education. Her particular research interests are in areas of pre-school teaching and curriculum, play and learning. Her other research interest is in the relationship between education and culture and tradition. She is a member of the CiCe Steering Group.

Panayota Papoulia-Tzelepi was, until she retired in 2004, professor in the Department of Elementary Education in the University of Patras (Greece). Dr. Papoulia-Tzelepi also served as vice-president of the Greek Pedagogical Institute (the Hellenic Ministry of Education and Religious Affairs, Athens) between 2001-2004. She was a member of the steering group of CiCe from 1998 to 2002, and since then has been a member of the CiCe MA development team. She is the Greek national coordinator for CiCe from 2004.

Marjanca Pergar Kuščer received her Ph.D in psychology from the University of Ljubljana in 1999. She is assistant professor of developmental psychology in the Department of Basic Education Studies at the University of Ljubljana (Slovenia), Faculty of Education, where she contributes to both undergraduate and postgraduate teacher training programmes. Her main areas of research are primary school teacher education, the developmental needs of children in school, cross-cultural comparison, values, the creativity of teachers and pupils, equal educational opportunities, the development of identity and conceptual development. She has participated in a variety of international and national research projects.

Simona Prosen is an assistant of developmental psychology at the Faculty of Education Koper, University of Primorska (Slovenia). She is interested in the field of self-concept, attachment, cognitive styles and cross-cultural psychology research. She also participated in neuro-psychological studies and in studies about the victimisation of women and substance abuse treatment.

Alistair Ross is professor of education at the London Metropolitan University (UK), where he is the director of the Institute of Policy Studies in Education and the international coordinator for the CiCe (Children's Identity and Citizenship in Europe) Thematic Network. His research interests are in the area of the school curriculum (*Curriculum: Construction and Critique*, Falmer, 2000), children's social and political learning, the careers of teachers (co-editor, *The Crisis in Teacher Education*, Trentham, 2002), citizenship education, and access to higher education (co-author, *Higher Education and Social Class*, Falmer/Routledge, 2003). He is series editor for *European Issues in Children's Identity and Citizenship*.

Maggie Ross is head of an Early Years Centre in inner London (UK), and formerly a senior lecturer in Early Years Education at what is now London Metropolitan University. She is particularly interested in the training of early childhood educators to work in multilingual and multi-cultural communities. She has also previously worked in primary schools and in a university department of education. She has written about young children's bilingual learning, early writing and early years educator's careers. She was formerly a member of the CiCe Early Years Group.

Nicos C. Sifakis is a lecturer in Applied Linguistics and Teaching English to Speakers of Other Languages (TESOL) in the School of Humanities of the Hellenic Open University (Greece). He is co-founder and coordinator of the ESP Special Interest Group of TESOL Greece. His research interests and publications are in the areas of English as an international language, adult education, teacher training and English for Specific Purposes (ESP).

Julia A. Spinthourakis is a faculty member of the Department of Elementary Education of the University of Patras (Greece). She is an assistant professor specialising in multilingual/multicultural education. Her interests and publications are in the area of second language teaching, social studies, teacher beliefs and culture in communication and the classroom.

Hugo Verkest is a lecturer in the School of Education in the Torhout campus of the Katholieke Hogeschool Zuid-West-Vlaanderen (KATHO) and a senior lecturer in methodology in the Higher Episcopal Institute of Education in Brugge (HIVO-Brugge) (Belgium). He has written textbooks on religion and ethics for primary and secondary school pupils, and was co-editor of the journal *Korrel*. He is currently teaching student teachers about visual literacy in Christian and contemporary art, and courses on visual data about poverty, sustainable development and conflict resolution He is international coordinator of KATHO (for primary education), national CiCe coordinator for Belgium and for EFTRE (the European Forum for Teachers in Religious Education).

References

Abbis-Chace, C. and Diaz-Bosetti, C. (2002) *Les plus belles comptines espagnoles.* Paris: Didier Jeunesse

Addo, A. O. (2001) Children's' idiomatic expressions of cultural knowledge, in Paechter, C., Edwards, R., Harrison, R. and Twining, P. (eds) *Learning, Space and Identity.* London: Paul Chapman/Open University. pp 57-66

Ainsworth, M. D. S. (1991) Attachment and other affectional bonds across the life cycle, in Parkes, C. Stevenson-Hinde, J. and Marris, P. (eds) *Attachment across the life-cycle.* New York NY: Routledge. pp 33-51

Ainsworth, M., Blehar, M., Waters, E., and Wall, S. (1978) *Patterns of attachment: A psychological study of the strange situation.* Hillsdale NJ: Lawrence Erlbaum Associates

Alexander. R. (2000) *Culture and Pedagogy: International comparisons in primary education.* Oxford: Blackwell

Almeida, M. V. (1991) Leitura de um Livro de Leitura: A Sociedade Contada às Crianças e Lembrada ao Povo in. O'Neil, B. J. and de Brito, J. P. (eds) *Lugares de Aqui: Actas do Seminário 'Terrenos Portugueses'.* Lisboa: D. Quixote. pp 245-261

Althusser, L. (2000) Ideology interpellates individuals as subjects, in du Gay, P., Evans, J. and Redman, P. (eds) *Identity: A Reader.* London: Sage. pp 31-38

Amir, L. B. (2004) *Homo Risibilis: Philosophy, Humor and the Human Condition.* Albany NY: State University of New York Press

Antone, R. and Mortier, F. (1997) *Socrates op de speelplaats. Filosoferen met kinderen in de praktijk.* Leuven:Acco

Anyon, J. (1979) Ideology and United States History Textbooks. *Harvard Educational Review,* 49, 3. pp 361-386

Appadurai, A. (1996) *Modernity at large. Cultural dimensions of globalization.* Minneapolis, MN: University of Minnesota Press

Apple, M. W. (1986) *Teachers and Texts: A Political Economy of Class and Gender Relations in Education* (2nd ed). New York NY: Routledge

Arleo, A. (1999) Syllabes Actes des IIièmes journées d'études linguistiques, Nantes: Université de Nantes

Arleo, A. (2003) Le folklore peut-il contribuer à la sensibilisation précoce aux langues étrangères? *Colloque international: Les enjeux d'une sensibilisation très précoce aux langues étrangères en milieu institutionnel.* Nantes: Université de Nantes

Arthur, N. (2001) Using critical incidents to investigate cross-cultural transitions. *International Journal of Intercultural Relations,* 25, pp 41-53

Ashmore, R. D., Deaux, K., and McLaughlin-Volpe, T. (2004) An organizing framework for collective identity: Articulation and significance of multidimensionality. *Psychological Bulletin,* 130, 1. pp 80-114

Barca, I. and Fonte, A. . (1989) A Representação do Álcool nos Livros de Leitura do Ensino Primário. *Revista Portuguesa de Educação,* 2, 2. pp 95-105

Barreno, M. I. (1982) *O Falso Neutro.* Lisboa: Instituto de Estudos para o Desenvolvimento

Baumeister, R. F., and Leary, M. R. (1995) The need to belong. *Psychological Bulletin,* 117, 3. pp 497-529

Bento, M. da C. R. L. (1999) Concepções de alunos e professores sobre o manual escolar de Língua Materna, in Castro, R.V., Rodrigues, A., Silva, J. L. and. de Sousa, M. L. D. (eds) *Manuais Escolares: Estatuto, funções, história. Actas do I Encontro Internacional sobre Manuais Escolares.* Braga: Centro de Estudos em Educação e Psicologia/Instituto de Educação e Psicologia da Universidade do Minho. pp 111-120

Berk, L. E. (1994) *Child development.* Boston MA: Allyn and Bacon

Bivar, M. de F. (1975) *Ensino Primário e Ideologia* (2nd ed). Lisboa: Seara Nova

Blackledge, A. and Pavlenko, A. (2001) Introduction to Special Issue: Negotiation of identities in multilingual contexts. *The International Journal of Bilingualism,* 5, 3. pp 243- 257

Boeve, L. (1999) *Onderbroken traditie.heeft het christelijk verhaal nog toekomst?* Kapellen: Pelckmans

Bourdieu, P. (1991) *Language and symbolic power.* Cambridge: Polity Press

Brandão, E. (1979) *Estereótipos em Manuais Escolares: Esboço Sociológico sobre a Dis-criminação Sexual nos Programas de Aprendizagem de Leitura.* Lisboa: Comissão da Condição Feminina

Bredella, L. (2003) For a flexible model of intercultural understanding, in Alred, G., Byram, M. and Fleming, M. (eds), *Intercultural experience and education.* Clevedon: Multilingual Matters, 31-49

Brenifier, O. (2001) *L'Apprenti Philosophe: L'art et le beau,* Paris: Editions Nathan

Brenifier, O. (2002a) *Enseigner par le débat.* Rennes: CRDP de Bretagne

Brenifier, O. (2002b) *L'Apprenti Philosophe: l'Etat et la Société,* Paris: Editions Nathan

Brown, B. (1998) *Unlearning discrimination in the early years.* Stoke-on-Trent: Trentham Books

Brown, G. and Yule, G. (1983) *Discourse analysis,* Cambridge: Cambridge University Press

Brumfit, C. (1984) *Communicative methodology for language teaching.* Cambridge: Cambridge University Press

Bruner, J. (1982) The organization of action and the nature of the adult-infant transaction, in Tronic, E. (ed) *Social interchange in infancy: Affect, cognition and communication.* Baltimore MD: University Park Press. pp 23-35

Bruner, J. (1990) *Acts of meaning.* Cambridge, MA: Harvard University Press

Bruner, J. (1996) *The culture of education.* Cambridge, MA: Harvard University Press

Bulckens, J. (1997) *Handboek voor godsdienstdidactiek* (2nd ed). Leuven: Acco

Bulckens, J. (2003) *Zin in leven.* Leuven: Acco

Burnett, C. and Myers, J. (2002) 'Beyond the frame': exploring children's literacy practices. *Reading literacy and language,* 36, 2. pp 56-62

Bustarret, A. (1986) *La mémoire enchantée, pratique de la chanson enfantine de 1850 à nos jours,* Paris: Enfance Heureuse Les éditions Ouvrières

Byram, M. (1998) Language teaching and education for citizenship, in J. Ciglar-Žanić, D. Kalogjera and J. Jemeršić, J. (eds) *British Cultural Studies: Cross-Cultural Challenges – IV. Language Learning as Cultural Learning: Approaches.* Zagreb: British Council. pp 347-358

Byrnes, J. (1998) *The nature and development of decision making: A self-regulation model.* Hillsdale, NJ: Erlbaum

Calvet, L-J. (1984) *La tradition orale*, Paris: Presses Universitaires de France

Canagarajah, A. S. (1999) *Resisting linguistic imperialism in English teaching*. Oxford: Oxford University Press

Canale, M. (1983) From communicative competence to communicative language pedagogy, in Richards, J. C. and Schmidt, R. W. (eds) *Language and communication*, New York: Longman

Canale, M. and Swain, M. (1980) Theoretical bases of communicative approaches to second language teaching and testing. *Applied Linguistics*, 1, pp 1-47

Carr, M. (2001) *Assessment in Early Childhood Settings: learning stories*. London: Paul Chapman

Castro, R.V., Rodrigues, A., Silva, J. L. and Sousa, M. L. D. de (eds) (1999) *Manuais Escolares: Estatuto, funções, história. Actas do I Encontro. Internacional sobre Manuais Escolares*. Braga: Centro de Estudos em Educação e Psicologia/Instituto de Educação e Psicologia da Universidade do Minho

Chambers, J. (1995) *Sociolinguistic theory*. Oxford: Blackwell

Chamot, A. U. and El-Dinary, P. B. (1999) Children's learning strategies in language immersion classrooms. *The Modern Language Journal*, 83 .3. pp 319-338

Chen, S., Chen, K. Y., and Shaw, L. (2004) Self-verification motives at the collective level of self-definition. *Journal of Personality and Social Psychology*, 86, 1. pp 77-94

Chew, P. G. L. (1999) Linguistic imperialism, globalism, and the English language. *AILA Review*, 13. pp 37-47

Chopin, A. (1992) *Manuels Scolaires: Histoire et Actualité*. Paris: Hachette

Chrisholm, L., Büchner, P., Krüger, H.-H., and Bois-Reymond, M. (eds) (1995) *Growing up in Europe: Contemporary Horizons in Childhood and Youth Studies*. Berlin: Walter de Gruyer

Chryssochoou, X. (2000) The representation(s) of a new superordinate category. *European Psychologist*, 5, 4. pp 269-277

CIDREE (Consortium of Institutions for Development and Research in Education in Europe) (ed) (1994) *The role of educational materials in curriculum process and internationalisation*. Report of CIDREE Workshop, Oslo, 30-31 May. Dundee: Scottish Consultative Council on the Curriculum

Cook, V. (1991) The poverty of stimulus argument and multicompetence'. *Second Language Research*,7, pp 103-117

Correia, A. F. and Ramos, M. A. de A. D. (2002) *Representações de género em manuais escolares. Língua Portuguesa e Matemática: 1º ciclo*. Lisboa: Comissão para a Igualdade e para os Direitos das Mulheres/Presidência do Conselho de Ministros

Cortesão, L. (1982) *Escola, Sociedade: Que Relação?* Porto: Afrontamento

CRESAS (2004) (Centre de recherche de l'éducation spécialisée et de l'adaptation scolaire) (Institut National de Recherche Pédagogique), at http://www.inrp.fr/

Crystal, D. (1997) *English as a global language*. Cambridge: Cambridge University Press

da Bento, M. C. R. L. (1999) Concepçõe9s de alunos e professores sobre o manual escolar de Língua Materna, in Castro, R., Rodrigues, A., Silva, J. and de Sousa, M. (eds) *Manuais Escolares: Estatuto, funções, história. Actas do I Encontro Internacional sobre Manuais Escolares*. Braga: Centro de Estudos em Educação e Psicologia/Instituto de Educação e Psicologia da Universidade do Minho. pp 111-120

Damasio, A. (2000) *Tapahtumisen tunne: Miten tietoisuus syntyy*. Helsinki: Terra Congita Oy

Day, E. M. (2002) *Identity and the young English language learner.* Clevedon: Multilingual Matters

De Bruyne, E. (1940) *Philosophie van de kunst, Phaenomenologie van het kunstwerk,* Antwerpen -Brussel: Standaard Bekhandel

Demetriou, A. (2003) Mind, self, and personality: dynamic interactions from late childhood to early adulthood'. *Journal of Adult Development,* 10, 3. pp 151-171

Denmark *The Folkeskole Act* (LBK.nr. 870 of 21 October 2003) www.uvm.dk

Denmark (2004) *Social Services Act, Lovforslags-udkast* (www.socialministeriet.dk)

Denmark, Ministry for Integration (2004) *Welcoming the newcomers* (www.inm.dk)

DfEE [Department for Education and Employment] (2000) *Curriculum guidance for the foundation stage.* London: DfEE, London

Dolto, F. (1995) *When Parents Separate.* Lincoln, MA: Godine

Dowling, M. (2001) *Young children's personal, social and emotional development.* London: Paul Chapman

Driscoll, M. P. (1993) *Psychology of learning for instruction.* Boston MA: Allyn and Bacon

Dumont, L. (1980) *On Value. The Proceedings of the British Academy,* 66, pp 207-41

Dumont, L. (1985) *Homo Aequalis.* Paris : Gallimard

Dýrfjord, K. (2001a) Hver hefur skilgreiningarvaldid i leikskolanum? [Who has the right to define in the Pre-school?] *Athöfn,* 1

Dýrfjord, K. (2001b) The national curriculum for Icelandic Pre-school, in Ross, A (ed) *Learning for democratic Europe.* London: CiCe. pp 69-74

Dyrfjord, K. (2001c) Umonnun eda skolun, hvort er mikilvaegara i leikskola? (Caring or instruction, what is more important in Pre-schools?) *Reggiofréttir* 2, 3. pp. 3-11

ECEF [Early Childhood Education Forum] (1998) *Quality and diversity in early learning.* London: ECEF, National Children's Bureau

Eco, U. (2003) *Venus unveiled,* exhibition with Omar Calabrese, Palais des Beaux-Arts, Brussels, 11 October 2003 – 11 January 2004

Edwards, D. and Mercer, N. (1987) *Common Knowledge: The development of understanding in the classroom.* London: Methuen

Edwards, D. and Potter. J. (1992) *Discursive Psychology.* London: Sage

Eidelson, R. J, and Eidelson, J. I. (2003) Dangerous ideas: five beliefs that propel groups toward conflict. *American Psychologist,* 58, 3. pp 182-192

Elias, N. (2000) Homo clauses and the civilizing process, in du Gay, P., Evans, E. and Redman, P. (eds) *Identity: A Reader.* London: Sage publications. pp 284- 296

Elliot, D. L., and Woodward, A. (eds.) (1990) *Textbooks and schooling in the United States: Eighty-nine yearbook of the National Society for the Study of Education.* Chicago, IL: NSSE/University of Chicago Press

Ellis, R. (1997) *The study of second language acquisition.* Oxford: Oxford University Press

Eppler, M. A. (1995) Development of Manipulatory Skills and the Development of Attention. *Infant Behavior and Development,* 18, pp 391-405

Erasmus of Rotterdam (1979) De Pueris, in Miller, C, (ed) *Erasmi opera omnia,* Vol 13, Amsterdam: North-Holland Publishing Company

Erwin, P. G. (1985) Similarity of attitudes and constructs in children's friendships. *Journal of Experimental Child Psychology,* 40. pp 470-485

EURYDICE (2002) *Key competencies. A developing concept in general compulsory education.* Brussels: EURYDICE

Favret, H. and Lerasle, M. (2001) *A l'ombre de l'Olivier, le Maghreb en 29 comptines,* Paris: Didier Jeunesse

Fernandes, J. V. (1987) *A Escola e a Desigualdade Sexual.* Lisboa: Livros Horizonte

Feyerabend, P. K. (1975) *Against Method.* New York NY: Verso

Fox, C. (1997) The authenticity of intercultural communication. *International Journal of Intercultural Relations,* 21, 1. pp 85-103

Freitas, M. L. A. V. de (1999) Funções dos manuais de Estudo do Meio do 1° ciclo do ensino básico, in Castro, R. Rodrigues, A., Silva, J. and de Sousa, M. (eds) *Manuais Escolares: Estatuto, funções, história. Actas do I Encontro Internacional sobre Manuais Escolares.* Braga: Centro de Estudos em Educação e Psicologia/Instituto de Educação e Psicologia da Universidade do Minho. pp 241-254

Freitas, M. L. A. V. de (2000) Textbooks and citizenship education. in Ross, A. (ed) *Developing Identities in Europe.* London: CiCe. pp 253-256

Gaine, C., Hällgren, C. Domínguez, S. P., Noguera, J. S. and Weiner, G. (2003) 'Eurokid': an innovative pedagogical approach to developing intercultural and anti-racist education on the Web. *Intercultural Education,* 14, 3. pp 317-329

Gardner, H. (1983) *Frames of Mind, The Theory of Multiple Intelligences.* London: Harper Collins

Gardner, H. (1993) *Multiple Intelligences: The theory in practice.* New York NY: Basic Books

Giddens A. (1982) *Sociology: a brief but critical introduction* (2nd ed). London: Macmillan

Giddens, A. (1993) *Modernity and Self-Identity.* London: Polity

Giroux, H. (1992) *'Border crossings.' Cultural workers and the politics of education.* New York: Routledge.

Greve. A. (1994) Førskolelærerens historie i Norge 1920-1965. Fremveksten av en fagforening. Hovedfagsoppgave i barnehagepedagogikk 1992. *Barnevernsakademiets skriftserie* nr. 1/94

Gronke, H. (2001) Was können wir im philosophischen Diskurs lernen? Elemente einer sokratischen Pädagogik, in Apel K.-O. and Burckhart H. (eds) *Prinzip Mitverantwortung. Grundlage für Ethik und Pädagogik.* Würzburg:Königshausen u. Neumann. pp 203-223

Grosleziat, C. (2002) *Comptines et berceuses du baobab, l'Afrique noire en 30 comptines,* Paris: Didier Jeunesse

Gudmundsson, G. (1949) *Barnavinafélagid Sumargjöf 25 ára 1924-1949.* Reykjavík: Barnavinafélagid Sumargjöf

Guilherme, G. (2002) *Critical citizens for an intercultural world – foreign language education as cultural politics.* Clevedon: Multilingual Matters

Gunnlaugsson, G. Á. (1997) Fátækralöggjöfin og íslenska fjölskyldan á 19. öld, in Hálfdánarsson, G., Guttormsson, L. and Gardarsdóttir, G. (eds) *Saga og samfélag : pættir úr félagssögu 19. og 20. aldar.* Reykjavík: Sagnfrædistofnun og Sögufé. p85-102.

Gunnlaugsson, G. Á. and Gardarsdóttir, Ó. (1997) Adstædur og adstada íslenskra ekkna um sídustu aldarmót , in Hálfdánarsson, G., Guttormsson, L. and Gardarsdóttir). (eds) *Saga og samfélag: pættir úr félagssögu 19. og 20. aldar.* Reykjavík: Sagnfrædistofnun og Sögufé. p313

Gustavsson, A. (2003) *Perspectives and Theory in Social Pedagogy.* Stockholm: Daidalos

Hagstofa Islands (2003) Statistics Iceland. 2003. Taken from website March 2003. www. hagstofan.is

Hammerly, H. (1991) *Fluency and accuracy: toward balance in language teaching and learning.* Clevedon: Multilingual Matters

Hansen, F. T. (2002) *Uddannelse 8/2002,* Undervisningsministeriet

Harré, R. (1998) *The Singular Self.* Thousand Oaks, CA: Sage

Harré, R. and Gillett, G. (1994) *The Discursive Mind.* Thousand Oaks, CA: Sage

Hatch, E. (1992) *Discourse and language education.* Cambridge: Cambridge University Press

Havel, V. (1994) *Toward a Civil Society: Selected Speeches and Writings 1990-1994.* Prague: Lidove Noviny

Hedegaard, M. (2003) *At være blive fremmed i Danmark.* Århus: KLIM

Heesen, B. (1996) *Klein maar dapper. Filosoferen met jongere kinderen.* Budel: Damon

Hegstrup, S. (2003) The New Character of Students in Europe. *European Journal of Social Education: A bi-annual periodical of FESET,* 5. pp 21-30

Hegstrup, S. (2004) How to welcome children with Islamic background, in Ross, A. (ed) *The Experience of Citizenship.* London: CiCe

Helenius, A. (2002) Roots of imagination. paper given to Fifth Congress of the International Society for Cultural Research and Activity Theory, 'Dealing with Diversity'. 18-22 June. Amsterdam: Vrije Universiteit

Higgins, C. (2003) 'Ownership' of English in the outer circle: an alternative to the NS-NNS dichotomy. *TESOL Quarterly,* 37, 4. pp 615-644

Hjartardottir, S. (2001) Toward reconciliation of work and family life: Parent with pre-school children in Iceland and The Netherlands. MA dissertation. (Unpublished) Hogeschool Maastricht

Hogg, M. A., and Williams, K. D. (2000) From I to We: Social identity and collective self. *Group Dynamics: Theory, Research, and Practice,* 4, 1. pp 81-97

Holliday, A. R. (1999) Small cultures. *Applied Linguistics,* 20, 2. pp 237-264

Horvat, L., and Magajna, L. (1987) *Razvojna psihologija (Developmental psychology).* Ljubljana: DZS

Howse, R. B., Best, D. L. and Stone, E. R. (2003) Children's decision making: the effects of training, reinforcement, and memory aids. *Cognitive Development,* 18, 2. pp 247-268

Hymes, D. (1974) *Foundations of sociolinguistics: an ethnographic approach.* Philadelphia PA: University of Pennsylvania Press

Iceland (1973) *Law on Pre-school Teacher College* (nr. 10 /1973) [Lög um Fósturskóla Íslands]

Iceland (1976) *Act of law regarding bulding and running daycare centers. 112/1976[(Lög um byggingu og rekstur dagvistarheimila fyrir born*

Iceland (1992) *Law in respect of children* (20/1992), [Barnalög]

Iceland (1994) *Act of Law regarding Pre-schools in Iceland. Number. 78/1994. [lög um leikskóla]*

Iceland (1995a) *Pre-school regulation* (225/1995) [Reglugerd um leikskóla]

Iceland (1995b) *Act on maternity/paternity leave and parental leave nr. 95/2000 [Lög um fædingar- og og foreldraorlof]*

Iceland (1999a) *National Curriculum for Pre-school.* [English version]. (1999). Reykjavík. Menntamálaráduneytid

Iceland (1999b) *Adalnamskrá leikskóla. 1999.* Menntamálaráduneytid. Reykjavík. [Icelandic National Curriculum for Pre-schools]

Ivanovitch-Lair, A and Prigent, A. (2003) *Ohé ! Les comptines du monde entire.* St-Germain-du-Puy: Rue du Monde

Jaeger, M. M. *Velfærd i Europa* 22/2002. Copenhagen: Socialforskningsinstituttets

Jakkula, K (2002) *Esineiden antaminen. Kehityksen peili ja kieltä ennakoiva sosiaalinen merkki 9-34 kuukauden iässä.* Oulu: Acta Universitatis Ouluensis E 52 http://herkules.oulu.fi/isbn95142665367

Jenkins, J. (2000) *The phonology of English as an international language.* Cambridge: Cambridge University Press

Jensen, H. (1998) *Offerets århundrede.* Copenhagen: Samleren

Jensen, V. B. (2002) *Nationale læreplaner. Børn og Unge,* 2

Johnstone, B. (1996) *The linguistic individual: Self-expression in language and linguistics.* New York NY: Oxford University Press

Kachru, B. B. (1985) Standards, codifications, and sociolinguistic realism: The English language in the outer circle, in Quirk, R. and Widdowson, H. (eds) *English in the world, teaching and learning the language and literatures.* Cambridge University Press, Cambridge. pp 11-30

Kankaanranta, M. (2002) *Developing digital portfolios for childhood education. Institute for Educational Research.* Jyväskylä: University of Jyväskylä

Kant, E. (1899) *On education.* London: Kegan, Trench, Trübner and Co

Katsillis, J. and Rubinson, R. (1990) Cultural capital, student achievement and educational reproduction: The case of Greece. *American Sociological Review,* 55, 2 pp 270 – 279

Kenner, C. (2000) *Home Pages: literacy links for bilingual children.* Stoke-on-Trent: Trentham

Key, E. (1902) *Barnets århundrede.* Copenhagen: Gyldendal

Kim-ju, G. M., and Liem, R. (2003) Ethnic self-awareness as a function of ethnic group status, group composition and ethnic identity orientation. *Cultural Diversity and Ethnic Minority Psychology,* 9, 3 pp 289-302

Kjær, H. (2003) *Comments on the Bill* (www.socialministeriet.dk)

Kobal, D. (2000) *Temeljni vidiki samopodobe (Basic aspects of the self-image).* Ljubljana: Pedagoški inštitut

Korhonen, R. (2002) Identity and pre-school education in Näsman, E. and Ross, A. (eds) *Children's understanding in the new Europe.* Stoke: Trentham Books. pp 109-122

Korhonen, R. (2004) Pedagogical drama play in six years old children's pre-school education. (Manuscript)

Kovačev, N. A. (1996) Identiteta med individualizacijo in kolektivizacijo (Identity between individuality and collectivism). *Psihološka obzorja,* 5, 3. pp 49-67

Kress, G. and van Leeuwen, T. (1996) *Reading images: The Grammar of Visual design.* London: Routledge

Krzywosz-Rynkiewicz, B., Holden, C., Papoulia-Tzelepi, P., Spinthourakis-Patras, J., De Fritas, M. L., Verkest, H., Pergar-Kuščer, M., Goscal, A. and Korhonen, R. (2001) Attitudes and identity: a comparative study of the perspectives of European children (1), in Ross, A. (ed) *Learning for a Democratic Europe.* London: CiCe. pp 93-102

Krzywosz-Rynkiewicz, B., Holden, C., Papoulia-Tzelepi, P., Spinthourakis-Patras, J., De Fritas, M. L., Verkest, H., Pergar-Kuščer, M., Goscal, A. and Korhonen, R. (2002) Attitudes and identity: a comparative study of the perspectives of European children (2), in Ross. A. (ed) *Future citizens in Europe.* London: CiCe. pp 339-351

L' Homme, C. (1998) Language connection. *UNESCO Sources*, 104. pp 10-12

Lacan, J. (1982) *Ecrits: A selection* (trans A. Sheridan). New York NY: Norton

Lane, J. (1999) *Action for racial equality in the early years: understanding the past, thinking about the present, planning for the future*. London: The National Early Years Network

Leal, I. (1979) *A Imagem Feminina nos Manuais Escolares*. Lisboa: Comissão da Condição Feminina

Leikskolar Reykjavíkur (2003) Taken from website, March 2003. www.leikskolar.is

Linder, D. (2004) The Internet in every classroom? Using outside computers. *ELT Journal*, 58, 1. pp 10-17

Lipman, M. (1991) *Thinking in education*. Cambridge: Cambridge University Press

Lloyd, B. T. (2002) A conceptual framework for examining adolescent identity, media influence, and social development. *Review of General Psychology*, 6, 1. pp 73- 91

Lo, A. (1999) Codeswitching, speech community membership, and the construction of ethnic identity. *Journal of Sociolinguistics*, 3. pp 461-479

Løgstrup, K. E. (1991) *Den etiske fordring* (2nd ed), Copenhagen: Gyldendal

Lourdes, M. and Bautista, S. (1997) *English is an Asian language: the Philippine context*. Manila: The Macquarie Library

Mahler. M. S. and McDewitt, J. B. (1982) Thoughts on the emergence of the sense of self, with particular emphasis on the body self. *Journal of American Psychoanalytic Association* 30(4), 827-848

Marcia, J. E., Waterman, A. S., Matteson, D. R., Archer, S. L., and Orlofsky, J. L (1993) *Ego identity: A handbook for psychosocial research*. New York: Springer-Verlag, Inc

Marques, R. (1997) *Escola, Currículo e Valores*. Lisboa: Livros Horizonte

Martins, M. de L. (1992) *Para uma Inversa Navegação: O Discurso da Identidade*. Porto: Afrontamento

Matos, S. C. (1990) *História, Mitologia, Imaginário Nacional: A História no Curso dos Liceus (1895-1939)*. Lisboa: Livros Horizonte

Mayo, G., del Pilar, M. and Lecumberri, M. L. G. (eds) (2003) *Age and the acquisition of English as a foreign language*. Clevedon: Multilingual Matters

McIleveen, R. and Gross, R. (2002) *Developmental psychology*. London: Hodder and Stoughton

McKay, S. L. (2002) *Teaching English as an international language: rethinking goals and approaches*. Oxford University Press: Oxford

Menezes, I., Xavier, E. and Cibele, C. (1997) *Educação Cívica nos programas e manuais do ensino básico*. Lisboa: Instituto de Inovação Educacional

Messaris, P. (1994) *Visual literacy: Image, Mind, Reality*. Oxford, Westview Press

Mey, J. L. (2001) *Pragmatics: An introduction*. Oxford: Blackwell

Ministério da Educação/Departamento de Educação Básica (1998) Organização curricular e programas – *1º ciclo do Ensino Básico*. Lisboa: ME/DEB

Ministério da Educação/Departamento de Educação Básica (2001) *Currículo Nacional do Ensino Básico Competências Essenciais*. Lisboa: ME/DEB

Mónica, M. F. (1978) *Educação e Sociedade no Portugal de Salazar*. Lisboa: Editorial Presença/Gabinete de Investigações Sociais

Muller-Hartmann, A. (2000) The role of tasks in promoting intercultural learning in electronic learning networks. *Language Learning and Technology*, 4, 2. pp 129-147

Musek, J. (1994) *Psihološki portret Slovencev (Psychological portrait of the Slovenians)*. Ljubljana: Znanstveno in publicistično središče

Näsman, E., von Gerber, C. and Hollmer, M. (1999) To share Children's Thoughts and Experiences, in Ross, A. (ed) *Young Citizens in Europe*. London: CiCe. pp 231-240

Nieto, S. (1999) *The light in their eyes: creating multicultural learning communities*. Stoke-on-Trent: Trentham Books

O'Dowd, R. (2000) Intercultural learning via videoconferencing: a pilot exchange project. *ReCALL*, 12, 1. pp 49-61

Opie I. and Opie, P. (1987) *The Lore and Language of Schoolchildren*. Oxford: Oxford University Press

Pais, J. M. (1999) *Consciência histórica e identidade: Os jovens Portugueses um contexto Europeu*. Oeiras: Celta

Paivio, A. (1986) *Mental representations: a dual coding approach*. Oxford: Oxford University Press

Pečjak, V. (1989) Misliti, delati, živeti ustvarjalno (Thinking, working, living creatively). Ljubljana: DZS

Pedersen, J. S. (2003) Sociologiens drøm – og mareridt. Politiken, Sektion 2, § 4 (21 November 2003)

Pennycook, A., (1998) *English and the discourses of colonialism*. Routledge: London

Pergar, K. M. (2001) Can the teacher's personality influence development of identity in pupils? in Ross, A. (ed) *Learning for a democratic Europe*. London: CiCe . pp 155-170

Pergar-Kuščer, M. (2002) Creative teacher – creative pupil, in Tatkovič. N. (ed) The 2nd Days of Mate Demarin, Brijuni 14th to 16th June. *High quality education and creativity: collection of scientific papers: international scientific meeting*. Zagreb: Croatian Pedagogical-Litterary Society. pp 159-166

Perner, J. (1991) *Understanding the representational mind*. Cambridge MA: MIT Press

Phillipson, R. (1992) *Linguistic imperialism*. Oxford: Oxford University Press

Piaget, J. (1951) *Play, dreams and imitation in childhood*. London: Routledge Kegan Paul

Piaget, J. (1977) *Psihologija inteligencije (The psychology of intelligence)*. Beograd: Nolit

Pikler, E. (1994) Peaceful Babies, Contented Mothers. Reprinted in *Bulletin of Sensory Awareness Foundation*. 14, Winter 1994

Pollard, A. (1985) *The Social World of the Primary School*. London: Holt, Rinehart and Winston

Pollard, A. and Filer, A. (1996) *The Social World of Children's Learning: Case studies of pupils from four to seven*. London: Cassell

Pollard, A. and Filer, A. (1999) *The Social World of Pupil Career: Strategic biographies through primary school*. London: Cassell and Continuum

Pollock, G. (1988) *Vision and Difference*. London: Routledge

Pollock, G. (2000) *Looking back to the Future: Essays on Life, Death and Art*. London: Routledge

Portugal (1986) *Diário da República* Lei nº 46/86 de 14 de Outubro de 1986 (Republic Daily, October, 14, 1986)

Portugal (2001) *Diário da República* Decreto-Lei nº 6/2001 de 18 de Janeiro (Republic Daily, January, 18. 2001)

Postman, N. (1994) *The Disappearance of Childhood*. 2nd edition. New York NY: Vintage Books/Random House

Praper, P. (1999) *Razvojna analitična psihoterapija 9Developmental analytical psycho-therapy*). Ljubljana: Inštitut za klinično psihologijo

Pratt, M. L. (1992) *Imperial eyes: Travel writing and transculturation*. London: Routledge

Pratt, M. L. (2002) Modernity and periphery: Toward a global and relational analysis in Mudimbe-Boyi, E. (ed) *Beyond dichotomies. Histories, identities, cultures and the challenge of globalization*. Albany, NY: State University of New York. pp 21-48

Radich, M. C. (1979) *Temas de História em Livros Escolares*. Porto: Afrontamento

Rampton, B. (1995) *Crossing: language and ethnicity among adolescents*. London: Longman

Refshauge, G. and Bak, S. (2001) *Tætte relationer*. Århus: Århus Kommune

Reich, E. K. (2002) *Frederik* (4th ed). Copenhagen: Gyldendal

Richards, M. and Light, P. (1986) *Children of Social Worlds*. Cambridge: Polity

Risse, T. (2003) The Euro between national and European identity. *Journal of European Public Policy*, 10, 4. pp 487-505

Robertson, I. (1989) *Society – A brief introduction*. New York NY: Worth Publishers

Rogoff, B. (1990) *Apprenticeship in Thinking: cognitive development in social context*. Oxford: Oxford University Press

Rosenfield, D. and Stephan, W. (1981) Intergroup relations among children, in Brehm, S. S. Kassin, S. M. and Gibbons, F. X. (eds) *Developmental social psychology*. New York: Oxford

Ross, M. (2001) Bilinguality and making learning possible in the early years, in Datta, M. (ed) *Bilinguality and literacy: principles and practice*. London: Continuum

Rudmin, F. W. (2003) Critical history of the acculturation psychology of assimilation, separation, integration, and marginalization. *Review of General Psychology*. 7, 1. pp 3-37

Ryan, A. M. (2001) The peer group as a context for the development of young adolescent motivation and achievement. *Child Development*, 72, 4. pp 1135-1150

Santos, M. E. V. M. (2001) *A cidadania na 'voz' dos manuais escolares: O que temos? O que queremos?* Lisboa: Livros Horizonte

Saran, R. and Neisser, B. (2004) *Enquiring Minds – Socratic dialogue in education*. Stoke on Trent: Trentham

Schmidt, L-H. (1998) Socialpædagogikkens genkomst. *Tidsskrift for Socialpædagogik*, 1, 12 p23

Schmidt, L-H. (1999) Dannelse på ny. *Dansk Pædagogisk Tidsskrift*, 1. pp 32 – 45

Schnitzer, E. (1995) English as an international language: implications for interculturalists and language educators. *International Journal of Intercultural Relations*, 19, 2. pp227-236

Schultz-Jørgensen, P. (2002) Den virkelighed børn lever. *Socialpolitik 5/6*

Sercu, L. (2002) Autonomous learning and the acquisition of intercultural communicative competence: some implications for course development. *Language, Culture and Curriculum*, 15, 1. pp61-74

Shen, J. (1994) Ideological management in textbooks: A study of the changing image of the United States in China's geography textbooks. *Theory and Research in Social Education*, 22 (2) pp194-214

Shi-Xu (2001) Critical pedagogy and intercultural communication: creating discourses of diversity, equality, common goals and rational-moral motivation. *Journal of Intercultural Studies*, 22, 3. pp279-293

Sifakis, N. C. (2004) Teaching EIL – teaching international or intercultural English? what teachers should know. *System*, 32, 2. pp237-250

Sifakis, N. C. and Sougari, A.-M. (2003) Facing the globalisation challenge in the realm of English language teaching' *Language and Education,* 17, 1. pp59-71

Sifianou, M. (2001) *Discourse analysis: an introduction.* Athens: Leader

Simões, J. M. F. S. (1987) Educating for passivity: A study of Portuguese education (1926-1968). Unpublished doctoral dissertation. University of London, Institute of Education

Singer, M. R. (1998) *Perception and identity in intercultural communication.* Yarmouth ME: Intercultural Press

Singh, P. and Doherty, C. (2004) Global cultural flows and pedagogic dilemmas: teaching in the global university contact zone. *TESOL Quarterly,* 38, 1. pp9-42

Siraj-Blatchford, I. and Clarke, P. (2000) *Supporting Identity, Diversity and Learning in the Early Years.* Buckingham: Open University Press

Siraj-Blatchford, I., Sylva, K., Taggart, B. Sammons, P., Melhuish, E, and Elliot,K. (2003), *Technical Paper 10 – The Effective Provision of Pre-School Education (EPPE) Project: Intensive Case Studies of Practice across the Foundation Stage.* London: DfEE / Institute of Education, University of London.

Skutnabb-Kangas, T. (2000) *Linguistic genocide in education – or worldwide diversity and human rights?* Mahwah NJ: Lawrence Erlbaum Associates

Smidt, S. (1999) *Planer og virkelighed.* Copenhagen: Gyldendal

Smith, L. (1976) English as an international auxiliary language. *RELC Journal,* 7 pp38-43

Smrtnik, V. H. (2004) *Custva in razvoj čustev. (Feelings and their development).* Ljubljana: Univerza v Ljubljani – Pedagoška fakulteta

Sommer, D. (2003) *Barndomspsykologi.* Copenhagen: Hans Reitzel

Spinthourakis, J. A. (2004) Unpublished paper at sixth conference of the Children's Identity and Citizenship in Europe Thematic Network, Krakow, Poland, May 2004

Spinthourakis, J. A. and Katsilis, J. (2004) The role of family in the formation of social identity in Krzywosz-Rynkiewicz, B. and Ross, A. (eds) Social learning inclusiveness and exclusiveness in Europe. Stoke on Trent: Trentham Books. pp11-19

Stables, A. (2003) Learning, identity and classroom dialogue, *Journal of Educational Enquiry,* 4, 1

Stalford, H. (2000) The citizenship status of children in the European Union. *The International Journal of Children's Rights,* 8. pp101-131

Stern, D. (1998) *De første seks måneder* (2nd ed). Copenhagen: Hans Reitzel

Stray, C. (1994) Paradigms regained: Towards a historical sociology of the textbook. *Journal of Curriculum Studies,* 26 (1) pp1-29

Surestart (2002) *Birth to three matters: a framework to support children in their earliest years.* London: DfES

Surestart (2004) *2002/03 Childcare and Early Years Workforce Survey: Day Nurseries and other Full-day Care Provision.* London: DfES

Tajfel, H. (1981) *Human groups and social categories.* Cambridge: Cambridge University Press

Tarozzi, M. and Bertolini, P. (2000) Children at the dawn of the Internet: exploratory research on current and potential use at home and in school. *European Journal of Teacher Education,* 23, 2. pp189-201

Ting-Toomey, S. (1999) *Communicating across cultures.* New York NY: Guilford Press

Toerisme Knokke-Heist (eds) (1983 – 2003) *Cartoons, Internationaal Cartoonfestival Knokke -Heist.* Leuven: Davidsfonds,

Tratnik, D. (2003) Sprejemanje razlik in drugačnosti v povezavi z nacionalno in evropsko identiteto (Excepting differences in national and European identity), Unpublished diploma work. University of Ljubljana, Faculty of Education

Trevarthen, C. (1998) The child's need to learn a culture, in Woodhead, M., Faulkner, D. and Littleton, K. (eds) *Cultural worlds of early childhood.* London: Routledge/Open University Press

Valente, M. O. (ed) (1989) Manuais *Escolares: Análise da situação.* Lisboa: GEP/Ministério da Educação

Valsiner, J. (2000) *Culture and human development.* London: Sage.

Van der Leij, A. (1994) De tragiek van het gesloten boek, in van Lierop-Debrauwer, H. (ed), *De kunst van het lezen,* Den Haag: NBLC. pp23-31

Veresov, N. (1999) *Undiscovered Vygotsky. Europäische Studien zur Ideen- und Wissenschafts-geschichte. European studies in the history of science and ideas.* Frankfurt am Main: Peter Lang

Verkest, H. (2001) Meer dan duizend woorden, *Trefdag* COV, Kortrijk

Verkest, H. (2002) Vuur brandt alleen op de plaats waar het ook brandt. *Narthex, de clash in de klas,* 2, 1

Verkest, H. (in preparation, September 2004) Cartoons, de 'missing link' in handboeken, *Renoveren,* 1, 5

Von Barloewen, C. (2003) *Anthrophologie de la mondialisation,* Paris: Editions des Syrtes

Vygotsky, L. S. (1986) *Thought and language.* Cambridge MA: MIT Press

Vygotsky, L.S. (1997) *The collected works of L.S. Vygotsky. The History of the development of higher mental functions.* New York NY: Plenum

Vygotsky, L.S. (1998) The Problem of age, in Rieber R. (ed) *The collected works of L.S. Vygotsky: Child Psychology.* New York NY: Plenum

Wade, R. C. (1993) Content analysis of social studies textbooks: A review of ten years of research. *Theory and Research in Social Education,* 21 (3) pp232-256

Weedon, C. (1987) *Feminist practice and poststructuralist theory.* London: Blackwell

White, S. and Buka, S. L. (1987) Early Education: Programs, Tradition and Policies in Rothkopf E. (ed) *Review of Research in Education.* Washington DC: American Educational Research Association. pp43-91

Winn, B. (1987) Charts, Graphs, and Diagrams in Educational Materials, in Willows, D. M. and Houghton, H. A. (eds), *The psychology of Illustration: Part 1 Basic Research.* New York NY: Springer Verlag. pp51-85

Wordsworth, W. (1888) *The Complete Poetical Works* ['The Rainbow', 1802] London: Macmillan

Yüksekkva, M. (2004) *Politiken,* January 12th 2004

Zupančič, M. (2004) Razvoj identitete in poklicno odločanje v mladostništvu (Identity development and vocational decision-making in adolescence). L. Marjanovič Umek in M. Zupančič (ed). *Razvojna psihologija (Developmental psychology).* Ljubljana: Znanstvenora-ziskovalni inštitut Filozofske fakultete

Index

179